To John Nebell
in hope that some reading
pleasure will be found in these
pages   Sincerely,
          Hugh Downs

Yours truly

HUGH DOWNS

Yours Truly

HUGH DOWNS

HOLT, RINEHART AND WINSTON
New York

COPYRIGHT © 1960 *by* HUGH DOWNS

*All rights reserved, including the right to
reproduce this book or portions thereof in any form.*

Published simultaneously in Canada by
HOLT, RINEHART AND WINSTON OF CANADA, LIMITED

FIRST EDITION

Acknowledgments

The author wishes to express his thanks and appreciation to the authors and publishers who have granted permission to use selections from the following published works:

"Fern Hill" from *The Collected Poems of Dylan Thomas*, copyright 1952, 1953 by Dylan Thomas. Reprinted by permission of New Directions and J. M. Dent and Sons, Ltd.; "Ode in Time of Hesitation" by William Vaughn Moody from *Poems of American History*. Reprinted by permission of Houghton Mifflin Company; *Newsweek*, October 26, 1959, "TV's Big Question: What is Morality?"; *The Meeting of East and West* by F. S. C. Northrop, copyright 1946 by The Macmillan Company; *Newsweek*, October 26, 1959, "TV's Big Question: What is Morality?" from a quotation by Rod Serling.

Library of Congress Catalog Card Number 60-12317
38460
PRINTED IN THE UNITED STATES OF AMERICA

This book is dedicated to three women:
Edith Downs, Ruth Downs, Deirdre Downs,
*for my inherited outlook, my inspiration,
and my challenge*

NOTE

*Any resemblance to persons
living or dead
is probably because there are such people*

Contents

	Introduction	xi
1.	*The Shot's on Me*	1
2.	*First Trip to Flubdom*	9
3.	*Malevolence or Mental Myopia?*	16
4.	*The Green and Golden Days*	21
5.	*If All the World Were Mechanized*	35
6.	*Chicken à la Downs*	47
7.	*Talent, Tenacity and Trowels*	56
8.	*Stage Fright: Innocence or Arrogance?*	62
9.	*TV Technique—The Unknown Quantity*	73
10.	*Two Boys and a Still*	88
11.	*Take a Giant Step*	100
12.	*Ben Dougherty*	113
13.	*Hi Jinx and Happenstance*	123
14.	*First Impressions*	133
15.	*Catastrophes and Stiff Upper Lips*	140
16.	*The Ad Game*	148
17.	*Our Daily Bread*	161
18.	*A Deal with Reality*	173
19.	*What is Anybody Really Like?*	187
20.	*Cogitations of a Broadcaster*	195

Introduction

IN A DISCUSSION on the Jack Paar show in the spring of 1959 I was asked what I thought of progressive education. I said I believed progressive education was a manifest failure and that it was asinine. I take no particular pride in this answer—as a matter of fact it's lacking a little in dignity—but it said what I feel, and if I were called on to restate it, I would say I believe progressive education is a manifest failure and that it *is* asinine.

Within hours I had stacks of wires and within days, a flood of mail lauding and condemning my attitude. It ranged from maudlin reactionary praise to thoughtful pleas that I re-read Dewey's *Schools of Tomorrow*. It came from people whose children were in serious difficulty in schools which have thrown out all old-fashioned teaching methods, and with them, much that was good and essential to disciplined learning. It came in threatening blasts from chronic malcontents who defend anything (however chaotic) which does away with any method tainted by tradition. In short, it came from both sides and ranged in the case of each side from literate essays to crank abuse.

I learned from this response that there was far more reaction to a comment on education than I would have guessed, and that on this issue those in sympathy with my opinion were apparently as prone to write as those critical of it. This is not usually the case, and I think it means America is more deeply concerned on the citizen level about its present education picture than legislators and bodies of officialdom are aware.

The incident made me think. Why, I asked myself, have I the opportunity to give an opinion so casually, and have it amplified so that a nation can hear it and comment on it? Have I the right to do this?

There is no question of my right to speak freely. The question is, has anyone the right even for a minute to take a broadcast channel belonging to the public and sound off in a voice many millions of times louder than the one nature gave him.

I think the right exists.

I do not think the question has to do with rights. Merely that it happens makes it a fact to be dealt with, and the question is of responsibility, not rights.

While it must be agreed that the television industry today is a giant whose influence is incalculable, it is, nevertheless, in its infancy. Those who have become enmeshed in the phenomenal growth of this gigantic infant are often too deeply involved to recognize the immaturity of the medium, assuming in the heat of daily pressures that they, along with TV itself, have arrived at the ultimate of importance and grandeur.

In my own view, we (meaning those who make up the television studio world) still have much to learn.

We have by no means "arrived," simply because we are not yet fully aware of the tremendous power we wield either for good or for evil. Nor have most of us come to the realization that we have a responsibility to use such vast power thoughtfully and, if possible, wisely.

For some time it has been my wish to set down the things I believe about broadcasting and its personalities, and in the course of doing so, to tell my own story as it relates in its small way to this fast-moving, fascinating world. From my vantage point on the Jack Paar show and others, I have seen public reactions which show the fantastic ability of masses of people to size up a situation with speedy and brilliant insight, and I see other reactions that prove you can still fool all the people some of the time and some of the people all of the time.

What the public sees on the screen is like the exposed portion of an iceberg. Supporting the pinnacle is a much greater mass, hidden from view below the surface. Behind the scenes—off camera—is a greater drama than anything flashed over the airways.

Just what is television and how does it fit the so-called American Way of Life? Is its function purely one of entertainment? A great many stars and producers seem to think so. Is it a vital communications medium? Watching Ed Murrow's "See It Now" or "World Wide 60" or other documentary productions, you gain a sense of TV's educational power. Perhaps it is both these things or many things rolled into one. In any case, its role in American life today is so important that we must accept it as a force in modern democracy.

If you believe in democracy, you believe the public knows what's best, at least in the long run. And if the public knows what's best, then it doesn't need arbiters of taste and morality, government-appointed or self-appointed, to determine its entertainment fare or to act as filters in its communication channels. In short, it doesn't need censors.

If the public doesn't need censors, then free-enterprise competitive broadcasting is the kind of broadcasting that will most surely improve itself, artistically, educationally and morally, because the public will give its loyalty to those shows and concepts which are the best, in the highest meaning of the word.

If you disagree with this concept of democratic controls, I would want to defend your right to do so. However, I would like to be sure that we aren't thinking of different definitions of the word "censor." Libel and postal laws, in my view, are not necessarily censorial, since they do not prohibit expression. Nor is the action of any "decency" type of organization which simply reviews and recommends for its own group. A network continuity acceptance chief, anxious to prevent offense that would ultimately result in a drop in viewing, is not a censor, for he is attempting to abide by public demand, and if he errs, he is soon forced to recognize his error by the public's reaction. But any person who prohibits, destroys, blocks, or impedes productions to satisfy his personal beliefs or prejudices while claiming his action is for the good of the public, is a censor.

Assuming that free-enterprise competitive broadcasting is best, the broadcaster who seeks longevity in his career will want an element in his broadcast technique that survives competition—an element that never gets stale, that can never be overexposed. This element is honesty.

For purely expedient reasons (if reasons of principle are not operative) the broadcaster who wishes to last will start with honesty as his foundation. He is therefore the keeper of a most sacred trust, to himself as well as his fellow citizens. To betray this trust is to open the door to censors and to lay a momentary blight on the democratic process.

What is honesty in broadcasting? To what extent can fact be distorted to convey truth? Who decides when tradition and technique abrogate the rules of honesty? How much "showbiz" can be injected without cheating viewers? What is honesty and dishonesty in drama? What is justified in advertising phrases?

I intend that, by the end of this book, in addition to having gone around all Robin Hood's outbuildings with illustrative anecdotes in support of my thesis, I will have answered all these questions and more.

Television appears, in one important way, to have its philosophic cake and eat it too. In reaching millions simultaneously, it is certainly a mass medium. But in reaching them individually, or at most in very small groups, it escapes some of the drawbacks of mass audiences, and is very like a personal contact between performer and viewer. The movie- and theater-goer gets dressed up and leaves his dwelling and sits in unrelaxed fashion amid others who have done the same thing. He brings a different and more formal type of receptivity than he uses at home watching TV. For one thing, he will expect a more private approach on the part of the broadcasting personality since his circumstances of viewing are more private. When he is spoken to confidentially by an announcer or a personality who has a message for him, he has a right to expect that that person is talking to *him* and not to millions. In this way TV has the impact of the prophet and the scope of the statesman.

Will Durant wrote that it is the tragedy of things spiritual that they languish if unorganized but are corrupted by organization. This may explain why philosophers and prophets have eschewed attempts to legislate good on a grand scale. Because people's reactions and opinions are different depending on whether they are part of a group or alone, TV may represent the first strong approach to the public with the advantages of mass dissemination technique plus the advantages of a private individual approach. It is certainly in order to consider it an important force.

H. D.

I
The Shot's On Me

"W<small>E'RE SHOOTING</small> you from straight ahead," an echoing voice rang out. Blinded by twenty thousand watts of Klieg lights and writhing in the heat, I shuddered and waited for the sound of shots. For one split second, I imagined that there was a firing squad in front of me and that their last act of mercy had been to place me in a position facing the sun so that I couldn't see the guns aimed at me. But at the end of the countdown I was reporting the news instead of falling over in a heap.

Everybody knows now, I suppose, that television scenes, like movies, are "shot," but this was back in the early days, and I was nervous anyhow.

My reaction to the expression "shooting" has never changed. I still cringe whenever I hear it, and many directors with whom I work have been considerate enough to substitute other phrases.

As might be expected, there is a good reason for my aversion to the term. It's a very simple one. I was shot once—and I didn't like it.

I have no idea what percentage of living humans can make such a claim, but having the skin broken by a pellet discharged from the muzzle of a firearm constitutes being shot, no matter how trivial the wound, and I am therefore one of those folks. Offhand I can think of only two celebrities who can qualify. They are Ernest Hemingway and Frank Costello, but I doubt if that will influence my writing style or my gambling ability as I'm not in their league. They both got it much worse than I did.

When I call up the picture of the house on the Spencerville road where I lived as a teen-ager, and stand as I always do when it comes to mind, one hundred feet southeast of it, I can see the screen door to the breezeway between the house and the summer kitchen. It happened just outside that screen door. I was fourteen and it was autumn. I think I had less than one second's warning.

Habits acquire polish with continued practice. I had developed a knack of throwing myself into the screen door from the inside and causing it to yield in spite of its inertia (it was a heavy one) fast enough to allow me to pass through without breaking stride. The door had a hook on it which was never hooked but once that I remember. My brother Paul had hooked it for no reason I ever found out, and I strode into it and discovered too late that it was not going to yield at all. Partially extruded through the screen as I was, I thought for a minute I'd fractured my pelvis on the frame.

Be that as it may, what happened on a certain November day made me wish the screen had been hooked again. Paul and I had started cleaning two chickens in the summer kitchen. For a twelve-year-old, my brother had an acute sensitivity to what he considered the proper way of doing things. Poultry dressing was one of his specialties. Although the raising and selling of chickens, ducks, and geese was a fairly commonplace business enterprise, not all of the ritual connected with preparing them for market or table was commonplace or without a certain originality. Paul's business acumen was considerable and quite New England in flavor. For example, his finishing touch on a dressed duck involved what he called "blowing it up." Putting the neck in his mouth, he'd blow air between the skin and the rest of the bird. The air stayed there and gave it an appearance of plumpness it had not had up to that time. There was nothing ethically shaky about this procedure, as the duck weighed the same as it would have otherwise, but the practice might be considered sharp, in that it destroyed his competition. He enjoyed the reputation of raising the fattest ducks in that part of Ohio until he got to overdoing it and rumor spread that they were diseased. "Damn duck's got a tumor," one patron said.

Some of the ritual was pure hokum and rather Mithraic in character as I look back on it. Instead of draining the blood from freshly decapitated fowl, Paul would spin it out by centrifugal force, holding the bird by the feet and whirling it. It was his contention that this was quicker, more thorough and more merciful, since fowl are known to be capable of living for a time without heads. That made sense, even if it gave the walls and ceiling of the summer kitchen the air of a bombed blood bank. But it eventually became my job to do the whirling. This was in order that Paul might leap into the spray shouting "Charge!" There is no way that this could have influenced the salability of his product, but it was important to him. So I would whirl, and he would leap about and cover himself with glory.

On this particular day Dad was home from work with an attack of the grippe. The ritual was up to the point of plucking. After we plunged the fowl in boiling water, it was whirled again and set upon with a vigorous peeling action, the feathers—and sometimes part of the skin—coming off easily. At this point I was dispatched to fetch the water. Our bucket was on the stove and near boiling. Dad was in the kitchen and near boiling himself, as someone had mislaid *The Saturday Evening Post.* "Stolen" was the word he used. He was searching in the icebox, having looked everywhere else in the house. "Bunch of packrats," he mumbled hoarsely. The *Post* in question was nailed to the garage door as an archery target. As it was badly perforated, I thought it best to say nothing. When Dad's throat was sore he was inclined to be surly.

There was still time before the water boiled to get the magazine down from the garage door and maybe bury it. I came out of the house to the cement porch adjoining the summer kitchen, then strode into the screen door leading to the drive. As I said, I wish it had been locked.

Just outside I turned to my right and in the next split second saw (1) a cock pheasant walk across the drive on the other side of the road (a continuation of our drive into the game preserve opposite our place), and (2) a hunter farther down the drive, visible from the chest up. The bird was on the crest of that road; the hunter was standing beyond, facing it and me.

When he brought the gun up I was looking squarely into the barrel. I suppose one reason for this is that he did not have a dead bead on the bird. Otherwise the pheasant should have blocked my view. Nothing blocked my view. I was turning and starting to drop, and I got pretty far around before I was hit. The pheasant came off better than I did.

As I heard the blast I felt as though a handful of small stones had been flung at close range, hard, at my back. It seemed at the time that my head was struck too. Actually I was hit by two buckshot, one in the side just at the lowest rib and the other at the left of the spine.

I stayed crouched for a moment, expecting the other barrel, and then when it didn't come, I looked around. The hunter was running up the drive toward me shouting, "My God! My God!" It was Mr. McCullough, who ran the Ohio Power Company substation at the junction of the Spencerville and Shawnee roads. His approach was a shambling canter, arms waving awkwardly and legs on the verge of buckling. He was an intense man who seemed always at the edge of a breakdown. Now he was really unglued. When he reached me he dropped the gun, grabbed me by both shoulders and shook me as though I had just let the air out of his tires. Actually he was trying to convince himself I was still alive. Every few seconds he'd stop shaking to croak, "Are you all *right*, boy?" and before I could answer he'd shake me again.

In the midst of this he stopped, looked past me, and the blood went out of his face completely. He nearly dragged me to the ground as he sank to it, gibbering. Even though it was broad daylight the look on his face stiffened my hair.

What he had seen was Paul coming through the door, his ritual bloodstains fresh on his white shirt and face. Paul said, "Hi, Mr. McCullough."

Behind Paul, Dad appeared in his robe, looking like an alcoholic symphony conductor and saying, "What happened? What's the ruckus? Go wash your face and change your shirt, Paul."

"I — I — shot him!" blubbered Mr. McCullough. "I want to give myself up!"

"Stand on your *feet*, man!" My father was always annoyed at scenes that threatened his dignity, although what dignity he thought he brought here to be threatened I don't know.

"I shot him! It was an accident, but that's no excuse!" Red veins laced the whites of the man's eyes as he kept pointing at Paul.

"I'm the one who got shot," I said.

"Why did you shoot them?" my father asked.

"I didn't shoot at them," Mr. McCullough spoke earnestly, still sitting on the ground. "I shot at a pheasant—and—is there a doctor close?" I think he was asking this for himself, for he closed his eyes and put the back of a hand to his brow.

"Turn around," Dad said to me. "Take off your shirt." Again to Paul, "Get inside and wash!" And again to McCullough, "Stand *up*, sir!"

While I started to remove my shirt, Paul turned to go in, tripped and fell at the door.

"He's dying!" gasped Mr. McCullough, scrambling to his feet and backing into a bush.

"He's not dying, he's clumsy," said my father.

"I'm the one—" I began.

"O Lord!" moaned the hunter, reclining in the Sabina juniper as if it were a rest board tilted to his favorite angle. "Get inside there, boy," he said to me, "and phone for a doctor."

"I'm the one that got shot. Why should I have to do the phoning?"

Paul rose slowly, coughing and clutching his stomach. He was beginning to play it for all it was worth, but was interrupted by a kick Dad delivered with poor aim at his right hip. As it was a complete miss, it must have annoyed Dad terrifically; the dignity involved was below zero. But it sent Paul into the house.

Dad turned to Mr. McCullough. "Would you get out of my shrub, please?"

"Is he all right?" Mr. McCullough asked, looking at the house.

"Yes," I said. "I'm the one—"

"You're not bad?" Dad asked me.

"I don't think so."

Dad was looking at my back. "You got one there." He picked at the wound and held out a buckshot. "Hardly penetrated. Is that welt on your side from a shot?"

"I think so."

He held up my shirt. There was one little hole near the center of the back and an inch-long streak like a pencil mark to the left and a little below.

"I guess you're okay. How do you feel?"

"Fine."

"I'm certainly sorry," Mr. McCullough said softly. "I wouldn't for the world have had this happen. Would you help me out of this bush?"

We got him standing, but I wouldn't have bet on how long he'd stay up unsupported.

"If you want to press charges, I'll go quietly," he said, swaying.

"There's no need for that," said Dad.

"Unless I get gangrene and kick the bucket," I put in. After a warning look from Dad, I kept quiet.

"Did you fire from across the road?"

"Yes. Right down there."

"You know that's a game preserve."

Mr. McCullough was silent a moment and then said, "I guess I'm the criminal type."

"Nonsense."

"No, I am. It's caught up with me at last."

"Well, you go on home and rest. Don't worry about it. Can you make it all right?"

"Yes. And I can't tell you —"

"Please don't. Just leave."

I think the scene was more painful to Dad, with his grippe and everything, than the shooting was to me. As Mr. McCullough disappeared down the drive and on to the road, Dad helped me on with my shirt. "It's cold out here. Go in and put some iodine on that spot." He squinted past me. "Is that a magazine on the garage door?"

I swallowed. "Yes. It's nailed there."

"Take it down. It looks like hell." When be bent over and picked up the shotgun, I thought for a moment he knew it was his *Saturday Evening Post* and was going to finish what Mr. McCullough had started.

"We'll take this over to him later," Dad was saying. "I could call him back but I couldn't stand it. Now, put a jacket on and take that magazine down off the garage door."

I grinned, partly in relief and partly because with his wild hair and bathrobe, and holding that gun, he looked as though he were on his way to a masquerade party as Daniel Boone in drag.

2
First Trip To Flubdom

THE REASONS people go into broadcasting are as varied as the reasons why some viewers prefer Westerns to variety shows or vice versa, and why they munch popcorn or peanuts while they're watching them.

There's a widespread belief that all professional broadcasters and performers in all phases of show business are extroverts—that they are answering a deep need to call attention to themselves. There is a basis in fact for this belief. It would be flattering to take the term at face value, since "extrovert" literally means one who finds his interests outside himself, and this is a healthy way to operate. But I think the term "extrovert" in this sense means "exhibitionist"—one who requires attention to defend an image of himself which he has set up to compensate for feelings of inferiority. And, alas, that is a factor in our business, undeniably. Statistically, at least, people in the performing end of broadcasting tend to be insecure.

But also statistically, their disorder is the most beautiful of human warps, for as a class, they also tend to sentimentality, generosity, superstition, liberality of thought, a strong sense of fairness and warmth of expression—and they would put mercy over justice. Their objectivity is most in danger when ideas conflict with the need for love.

How and why do these folks find their way into the limelight? There is a reason for each case, even if it's an accidental one. With most of them it is not accidental, although in many cases the reason may be buried. Mine is apparently buried—I can't find it. All I can find are two examples of reasons for *not* going into broadcasting, both of which prove that I, at an early age, hated the limelight.

When I was two years old, the Downs family moved from Akron, Ohio, where I was born, to Lima, then a little over thirty thousand in population. My brother, Paul, was an infant at the time of the move and my youngest brother, Wallace, was born in Lima when I was six. My two outstanding memories of the period between moving and starting school are of being stung by a bee and of running up a nine-dollar candy bill at Cribley's Grocery before a telephone call from Mr. Cribley to my mother put an end to what was making me the most popular kid in that half of town. Since I was not what you would call a born leader, my position of prominence decayed rapidly with the drying up of my credit.

I started in the first grade at Horace Mann School at the age of five. Because the building was so old that Horace Mann's father could have laid the cornerstone himself, the top floors were condemned. But I doubt if Horace Mann's father had anything to do with it. He would not have wanted his son's name on a building with such faulty planning.

I remember an excellent teacher that first year, a Mrs.

Hawkins, who had the rare knack of being at once strict and compassionate, commanding respect while holding popularity. I also remember the school principal, Mrs. O'Neil, a woman of formidable size and appearance, who put salt on bananas before eating them. My mother, who went with me the first day, left shortly before the morning recess. Mistaking this as a signal for my own dismissal, I followed her home. There I announced I thought school was going to be lots of fun, leaving so much good daylight for playtime and where were all the other kids in the neighborhood? In four minutes I was making my second entrance into Horace Mann School accompanied again by my mother, this time in front of the still-assembled class and amidst an exchange between my mother and Mrs. Hawkins.

"He thought it was all over!"
"Ah, isn't that cute? No harm done."
"He's really enthused about school."
"Of course he is. He's a nice boy."
"Well, he'll know after this. I explained to him."
"Don't think a thing about it!"
"Thanks again and so sorry to disrupt. . . ."
"Not at all."

I don't recall any feeling either of acute dismay or of great exhilaration at being the momentary center of attention. The idea came slowly to me that I had in some way flubbed it up, but there was no particular anguish, either.

The only real anguish I remember during that year was once when we all carried papers and magazines to school for some reason, and there was a prize for the most by weight. I was astonished when I failed to win, as I had lugged about a ton and a half of wet copies of *The Satur-*

day Evening Post and *The Woman's Home Companion* two blocks along Rice Avenue. They all came out of our attic, which ought to have been condemned, too. The arduousness of this task should have strengthened my moral fiber in the way that breaking the ice in the wash basin and slogging through neck-high snow a mile to school fits American boys for statesmanship, but it actually reduced my desire ever to do physical labor again. I must say that such desire on my part was by no means impressive prior to that time.

My best friend in school sat across the aisle on my left. I don't remember if we sat close together because we were best friends, or if it was the other way around. Since circumstance plays such a big role in forming our feelings, it was probably the other way around, particularly since you seldom have a best friend before the first grade. Up to then you have only your brothers and sisters and the kids next door, whom you sort of like, and the kids farther down the block, whom you hate.

In any case, I now had a best friend sitting next to me across the aisle on my left. His name was Joe Hodges, and he was much bigger than I was. I've seen him only once since we grew up. He is six feet tall today, which is strange because he was at least seven feet tall when we were in the first grade together. He had a long head; he seldom laughed or smiled, and when he did smile it was as though he were paying most of his attention to something else, or realized that levity must be temperate since we are, after all, mortal. He was thoughtful. I was surprised he grew up at all because that kind of child traditionally dies young.

Joe double-crossed me on occasion, though not viciously. I had traded a screen-door spring to another boy for a police whistle. It was a bad June for my parents, who could have coped with the excessive number of flies that got in the house (due to the disabled screen door) if their nerves hadn't been wracked by the police whistle on which I could belt out a sound of such urgency that anyone within hearing must have thought cornered bank robbers were just behind them ready to open fire. Between the swatting and the jumping, my folks kept in fine physical shape.

One day I carried the whistle to school. I discovered that I could blow on it without producing sound if I kept a finger on the slit at the top. The little ball inside, which gave the sound its tremolo, would flutter against my finger in delightfully rich silence. I leaned over to Joe and whispered.

"Try it," I said. He took the whistle and blew into it, holding his finger on the slot. Finally he leaned over to me. He looked as though he might be smiling inside.

"You blow it," he whispered, "and I'll put my finger on it."

I remained leaning over into the aisle as he reached his long arm out to place a finger on the whistle.

"Blow hard," he whispered, and I noticed that now he was smiling outside—a pale, long-faced smile.

I blew. Hard. Midway in the expulsion of the great lungful of air, Joe withdrew his finger from the whistle, and with a quick movement returned to face the front of his desk.

What happened is not easy to describe. Mrs. Hawkins had had her head down reading a book, and there was a vase of flowers on the desk in front of her. It was not her reaction and the resultant loss of the vase that alarmed me, since I had learned it was standard for adults to leap into real spasms when surprised by my police whistle at full blast—it was the children standing on top of their desks and bouncing off the blackboards that made me realize I was in a very nervous group.

I'll have to say Joe carried it off smoothly. His first move was to exhibit feigned surprise, and he followed quickly by pointing to me so the teacher would run no risk of miscarrying justice through directing what followed at the wrong child.

Now at this point, once again, I suppose that being the center of attention should have touched some responsive chord in my inner being and have revealed to me in a sudden flash of insight that it was my destiny to perform in public. I can recall no such revelation. On the contrary, I was inclined at that moment to wish that the whole school building would suddenly collapse or that some equally violent disaster might divert the group's attention from me.

The old hickory stick may have passed out of use too soon. There was an intimate teacher-pupil and person-to-person relationship in the use of this temporarily bruising wand that has gone from the American scene. When I was a first-grader, it had already become the thing to avoid corporal punishment and substitute something lastingly humiliating and deeply scarring—a note to the parents implying that maybe you weren't really fit for school after all.

After the police whistle had been confiscated, the whole thing was narrated to my parents in the note I had to carry home.

Mother and Dad were lenient, I thought.

"You're sure Mrs. Hawkins has the police whistle?" my mother asked at supper.

I assured her she had it in the locked drawer of her desk.

"She didn't say that if you behaved," my father asked, "she'd return it to you? Or anything like that?"

"I'm pretty sure I'll never see it again," I said.

"Well," Dad said, brightening, "we all do things we regret. I wouldn't feel too badly." He swatted another fly. "Let's all take a ride in the machine and pick up some ice cream for dessert, shall we?"

3
Malevolence or Mental Myopia?

AMONG THE show-business traits that carry over into broadcasting is a sense of responsibility that fits strangely into an otherwise gypsy mood. The broadcast, like the show, must go on. It has been observed by cynics that no one has yet come up with a valid reason *why* it must go on, but it seems to be a fundamental rule nevertheless.

This would appear to thrust on the performer an obligation that could be borne more easily by one whose temperament is of a steadier nature than that required by certain kinds of creative talent.

Is there a way of coping with this dichotomy of requirement, both in performing and in life itself?

There are people who drift through life with no apparent alertnesss whatever. Others, probably less secure, keep their methods perpetually honed and at ready, as if they must proceed with the utmost vigilance. Such people are notable for their clarity of thought and speed of applying rational machinery to problems as they arise.

But this alertness may fluctuate within a single individual. At times he will display considerable brilliance in thinking and at other times he will appear to be a boob. This is not entirely capricious. It can amount to a "selective mental myopia." The reason for it is found in the fact that while it is often necessary to face things with all the astuteness one can muster, it is also comforting to face them with real fogginess of mind.

I do this.

Sometimes I put on my mental glasses for sharp appraisal and decisive action. At other times I squint out at the world like a mole because it better suits my comfort. This is a terrible admission. But in a large sense I think people who do this are less prone to disintegrate under heavy pressure, and are able to escape the sterility of unremitting common sense, which stultifies intuition.

Sometimes I get caught with my glasses down, and in matching wits with a sharpie I am momentarily foggy, with the result that I take a drubbing. No serious harm has ever come to me this way, but the foible dates back to my early life.

One day, when I was in the second grade, a tour was organized for the entire Horace Mann School to go through the condemned floors above the classrooms—floors three and four. The first and second stories were in use, as was a musty, whitewashed basement at one end of which were the boys' and girls' rooms. These were opposite the furnace room—a mysterious place, dominated by an awe-inspiring boiler with immense white pipes like the arms of an octopus extending from its body to the ceiling. It was tended by Mr. Lapp, a janitor who wore droopy coveralls made even droopier by the heavy wrench he always kept in his back pocket. He was never seen on any of the upper floors.

I remember deciding that a tour of those top floors was not such a hot idea since they were condemned precisely because they might cave in if you went walking around up there. But they were going through with it—six classes guided by three teachers.

Joe Hodges leaned over from his side of the aisle to whisper, "I'm not going up there!" I was already thinking the same thing.

"Me either," I said, but couldn't see any way out of it. As a matter of fact the teacher had said, "Those who want to . . .," but I hadn't listened properly and thought it was a forced march. Finally, Mrs. Hawkins said, "Now do we all want to go? Let's see all the hands of those who want to see the old rooms upstairs."

Most hands shot up, mine among them. Then I slowly brought mine down with a great feeling of relief. I didn't have to go. I noticed half a dozen others with their hands down.

"All right," Mrs. Hawkins smiled. "Those of you who stay may do whatever you wish, but you must remain in your seats. You may color, look at your books, or practice writing your names. All those going form a line here by the cloakroom door."

The line formed. I thought they looked nervous, although there was some giggling. Had I been older it might have touched me to see those brave little things marching off like a children's crusade. As it was, they didn't seem little to me since I was the same size. I simply thought they were a pack of fools. As they left I leaned over to Joe.

"I'm glad we're smart," I said aloud.

"I'm not so sure we are," Joe said, his face even longer than usual.

Somehow Joe Hodges could drape a person with a sense

of impending doom merely by stating the sun was shining. It was the way he said it. My stomach went chilly.

"What do you mean?" I asked.

"Well," said Joe, "Those floors are rotten. Part of the time they're going to be right up there." He pointed upward and followed his long finger with the eyes of a medieval hermit resigned to Divine Punishment. "We're sitting right here." He indicated his desk and mine. "And we'll *be* sitting right here when they all come down, and I don't mean down the *stairs*."

"Gosh!"

"I'll say gosh! You ever get a whole school of kids and a whole ceiling on your head?"

"And the teachers, too," I added.

"And the teachers, too," Joe said, as though I hadn't said it. "Boy!"

"What'll we do?" Now I was worried.

Joe rested his long chin on his fist and thought. Finally he said, "Only one thing *to* do."

"What?"

"Everybody goes out when there's a fire drill, don't they? So we ring the fire bell."

I just looked at him. He stared back at me. "Not me." I said. "Mrs. O'Neil would kill us."

With his chin still on his fist Joe turned his stare to his desk top. "Take your choice," he said ominously. Then he cocked his head as though listening and looked upward again. I got out of my seat and made for the door. He followed me. One of the other boys stood up. "Where you guys goin'?" he called after us. We didn't answer, but I remember thinking we were going to save all those who stayed behind, as well as ourselves.

Out in the hall Joe wiped his palms on his trousers, then

grabbed the fire bell rod. I squinted while I started to put my fingers in my ears. After a tense moment, Joe let go of the rod.

"Look," he said, "can you reach this?" I tried it and could. He bobbed his head. "Good," he said, almost smiling, "you ring it, and *I'll* go to the door to make sure the outdoors is clear so everybody can have room out there."

This seemed reasonable at the time, and thoughtful. I realize now that Joe should have been jumped to the fifth grade, and I should have been returned to kindergarten.

I rang the fire bell while Joe checked on the outdoors. Presently I was in Mrs. O'Neil's office where she was saying, "But even if Joe was going to ring it, the fact is that *you* were *ringing* it. Joe wasn't anywhere near it!" I looked around for bananas and salt but didn't see any.

The main reason she was sore at me was because the sound of the fire bell had convinced the tour above us that the upper floors were about to buckle. They all came down to the lower floors in what amounted to a rout. Some of the kids said that two of the three teachers got back down ahead of their classes, muscling them out of the way. I was sort of proud that our teacher, Mrs. Hawkins, did not do this, and I thought even more of her when I learned she had sent the children down ahead of her in orderly fashion after saying good-by to them, adding that she thought a good teacher should go down with her school.

4
The Green and Golden Days

PROBABLY EVERY broadcaster who presents himself as a personality, and is not simply chained to written copy, finds truth in the idea that we are the sum total of our experiences; that the ability to recollect past experiences is something that must color every act we perform and every view we hold.

Shortly after my tenth birthday Dad rented a small farm three miles out of town. Memories of the eight years spent there have become a series of sense impressions paraded across a picture of the old MacBeth house where we lived in the summertime, with excursions where necessary into the mind's file of other remembered pictures, all mellowed and condensed, but probably not too distorted.

Some mechanism, like that which produces hope, deals with memory in such a way that the painful, the drab, the unpleasant is drossed out of events as they recede in time, and only the gold that remains is honored with easy recall. But it often warps the view and it gives rise to talk of the Good Old Days. While there may have been much good about the Old Days, it's hard to justify the conviction memory carries that all those days, or most of them, were gems of sunshine and happiness. It does seem those summers spun on through dozens of months nobody bothered to count till school started. It seems the temperature was always the same—hot, but not unbearably or even unpleasantly so. Only the old have that keen discernment which tips them off to a three-degree rise or drop of the mercury—partly because they have lost their tolerance of extremes, and partly because experience, which is bought with innocence, has made them old. Time can take credit for only half of aging.

In those golden days, it was never any time by the clock. It was only breakfast time and suppertime and time to get washed up and time to go to bed. It was, in the gold of memory, field and water and weed, always blue overhead, timeless and safe, to "trail with daisies and barley down the rivers of the windfall light."

This art of the mind, subtracting a slanted essence from the total memory and making it reality, is so strong that personal research into the mass of total facts (none of them ever discarded) finds the drab ones, the unpleasant and painful ones now iridescent in the radiance of that bias. Everything is flavored with it. Pain and alarm have undergone the alchemical change to heroism and zest, because the past is safe.

The historical researcher, carefully documenting details of the past, sniffs out those fragments which are commonplace, and therefore almost lost, because such fragments have the ring of authenticity. But his love of the subject, far from being daunted by exposure to unromantic, factual harshness, holds these pieces in a light of high romance and he loves them for that reflected light.

I remember that my schooling continued in an almost

literally one-room schoolhouse. It had two rooms. Because I had started at five on a split-year basis and had to slip back a grade or go forward a grade to get in step, I went ahead, skipping half of the fifth. To this day I can't work fractions. The only inconvenience this causes is when I'm asked to translate temperatures from Centigrade to Fahrenheit or vice versa, and that's not more than once every six years.*

In this school, in the same room and with the same teacher, I went through the sixth grade. It had its flavor.

Mornings were spent listening to Mrs. Coon read from the Bible and Zane Grey. In the afternoons we studied geography, spelling, arithmetic, and history. I don't recall any historical discrepancies in Zane Grey's writings, but had there been conflict with orthodoxy, the discrepancies would have been assigned to the history text since Zane Grey was canonical scripture.

Most of the children at this school were older than I was, no matter what grade they were in, because I was a year ahead and because most of them had failed a great deal. All but two of them, I remember, were bigger. Duane Felton was smaller than I was, although two years older, and this, I was told, was because he smoked or drank coffee, or both. If he smoked he never did it around school. Once I asked him if coffee tasted good and he said no. But the idea of associating shortness of stature with these vices was drummed into me so forcefully that to this day when I see a very big man light a cigarette the thought flicks through my mind that he is doing it to check his size, which might get completely out of hand if he didn't smoke. And occasionally I fancy I shrink slightly if I have more than two cups of coffee at a sitting.

* $F. - 32 \times 5/9\text{ths} = C.$ $C. + 32 \times 9/5\text{ths} = F.$

There was Mike Potts, a doughy-faced mountain of a lad who did not smoke or drink coffee. He chewed tobacco and drank whisky. Nobody knew his age for sure. It must have been five or six years more than mine. Mike was a boy of extreme treachery. His mood could change in three-tenths of a second from bumbling affability to blind rage. He tried to kill my brother Paul once when Paul tried to stop him from throwing zinc jar lids into the lake. Paul had been saving them to melt down and cast into sinkers. Mike said they might as well sink now and save him the bother of melting them down. He was one of the two criminals in the class.

The summer before we moved there, I'm told, Mike had seemed to get religion, and the community was impressed. It was further impressed when it realized he was urging whole families to attend services on Sunday in order that he might go through their houses and steal them blind. If there was anything likable about him he had it skillfully hidden.

One of my most vivid memories centers around Betty Strunk, a precociously voluptuous girl of fifteen. All her precociousness went in that direction with nothing left over for learning, for she spent three years in the third grade, two in the fourth, and this was her second time around in the fifth. She seemed well-adjusted because she was so familiar with the material. Now that I look back, I realize there was something incomplete in my attitude toward her. She was rather helpful to me on a couple of written tests, but in the main I had no use for her and regarded her as a big cow, my romantic attention going in its entirety to Edna Miller, who was only one year older than I was and quite flat chested. It was not that I was unaware of the earthy charms which seemed to explode from Betty, but there is a clean separation of sexual and romantic feelings at the age of ten, the latter rather spiritual and the former inarticulate and unconscious. So my mind and heart never responded to Betty in any way (and neither did anything else, actually) but I'll tell you later why the vivid memory.

One boy my age and about my size was named Billy Haas. He was the fourth of fourteen children and claimed he could not remember the names of the two youngest. Billy and I had quite a few adventures. Two of them centered around the other of the two real criminals in the class, Ed Dunlap. Ed, unlike Mike Potts, was not demented, but he was extremely undesirable to society. He was in some ways the oldest of all that old class, and he would have been the master-mind type but for his tendency to remain aloof from what he considered the bumpkin type, which was everybody else in the world.

We played Cops and Robbers and Cowboys and Indians like all other children, but Ed stood on the sidelines until he figured a way to make it different. He figured some dillies. One involved bringing real pistols to school. It started when he got hold of a twenty-two caliber target pistol and we let him be the leader. Soon other guns appeared, smuggled from unsuspecting fathers. I remembered that there was a thirty-two caliber short-barreled revolver in the lower right-hand drawer of the dresser in my parents' room. Next day at school I had my own real gun and every recess for about a week and a half we were snapping the hammers in imaginary fusillades at each other and biting the dust in rather glorious fashion. Kids with cap guns weren't allowed in the game. As Mrs. Coon didn't know the difference between a cap gun and the real goods, this might have gone on till I moved on to junior high school, but for Ed's inventive mind. He brought a box of shells to school one day. The first I knew about it was when a little knot formed around him at the road's edge while he loaded. For a moment I thought he was going to shoot the teacher and take over the school to instruct us in the fine arts of crime, but his first shot was in the air and his second was aimed at the glass crown of one of the filling station pumps across the road.

Some inner voice spoke clearly to me at this point, convincing me something bad was about to happen. We lived fairly near the school. By running across the back field and through an orchard, I was home in a few minutes, puffing upstairs to deposit the thirty-two under some handkerchiefs in the lower right-hand drawer of the dresser. I got out again without being seen, after which I ran back to school. My arrival was simultaneous with two deputy sheriffs who were followed within a minute by a city squad car and a state police patrol car, which were followed by Mr. Shappell's car. He was the County Superintendent of Schools, including one- and two-room schools. Mrs. Coon said she thought she was going to faint when they rounded up eight revolvers and a Belgian automatic. They were short the actual count. There should have been eleven, or at least ten without mine. One of the others showed up the next week because it was clogging the toilet, but I never found out what happened to the last one, which belonged to Morton Jewett.

Morton was a good-looking sensitive Negro boy, about two years older than I was, who lived in the section called Powerstown or "Parstown." On the surface he seldom appeared to be really interested in anything, but his actions sometimes showed a rare and deep concern. I had wanted a bicycle very much and had spoken to him of my dream of owning one. Once, on a dump by the railroad tracks, I found a rusted bicycle seat without padding. I told Morton I wanted to find other parts. When there were enough, I would put them together and have a bike, which he could use half the time, if he helped. Shortly after that his older brother gave him an old bike he had reconditioned. Morton rode it to school only once, when he offered to let me borrow it. I declined on the grounds that he'd just got it and anyway I'd have my own as soon as I gathered enough parts to build it. He maintained an interest in my project, bringing me pieces from time to time. Later I discovered that six parts he had "found" for me were parts he'd removed from his own bicycle. He was actually taking it apart.

He never got angry unless there was some unfairness involved, and I can't recall his ever thinking the unfairness was aimed at him. When we had the real guns he suggested to each of us that we not aim them straight at each other "just in case," which seemed to me a sort of sissified idea. But Morton was a friend—as good a friend as I can remember.

He got in trouble years later according to a news item my mother sent me. He had cracked somebody's skull with a chair at a wedding reception. There must have been some unfairness involved.

In 1951 Morton Jewett was killed in the crash of his motorcycle. The accident occurred on the Spencerville road within sight of the farmhouse where I had lived when we were going to MacBeth School together.

I've thought since how strangely circumstances force the divergence of lives of people who have known and understood each other, and how in a fraction of a lifetime they drift distances that would seem to need thousands of years. I have wondered if Morton Jewett would still be alive if some friend had had an incomplete motorcycle for which Morton could have supplied parts by dismantling his own.

The first adventure Billy Haas and I had really belongs to him, and for years I wished it had happened to me. But now I'm just as happy to have watched it from a safe distance. With the wind in our faces, we were hiking along the Erie Railroad tracks after school one fall day. Usually you can hear a train coming from quite a distance behind you, but if the wind is the wrong way, it's a different story. We came to the trestle across the Auglaize creek and got about to the midway point when we heard it—a freight train out of Lima that had settled on its run so that the engineer and fireman must have felt it unnecessary to keep their eyes on the tracks. Otherwise they would have sounded the whistle sooner than they did. We began to run. Although it wasn't more than a few yards to safety, the big danger was in not putting our feet squarely on the ties. The temptation to look back was irresistible; once or twice we yielded to it. The train was closer, but we still had time. Suddenly I realized I was running alone.

"Billy!" I yelled. He didn't answer. I had to look around, but it required a couple of seconds to time in advance the placement of my feet on the ties. When I finally looked I saw Billy a dozen feet back, facing the train and stepping over the rail onto the ends of the ties that hung out over the stream. I yelled again. He turned in my direction and waved me on. By now I had stopped. The train was nearly on the trestle, its whistle a continuous blast. Billy sat on the tie-end and swung himself around. "He's going to jump," I thought. With that I used my remaining time to cover the distance to the end of the trestle. As the freight roared by above, I rolled in the cinders down a rather long incline and into some water and thistles in the ditch below. The earth shook: a jet of steam from the cylinders momentarily blotted out the sun. After I had picked myself up, I made my way to the creek's edge amidst a shower of tiny cinders and smoke particles. The surface of the creek was unruffled. There was nobody in it.

"Billy!" I shouted. The train continued to thunder across the bridge, the trucks shrieking and pounding and the timbers groaning. I looked up to see whether the caboose was in sight. It wasn't, but Billy was. His hands eight inches from the rumbling wheels, he was hanging from the end of a tie. I remember feeling glad the wheel flanges were designed to go on the inside of the rail. I went back on the trestle and helped him up after the freight had passed, but we both nearly fell in the creek.

"It would have been simpler to jump in, wouldn't it?" I asked him.

"Hardly," he said. "I'd have been killed in the drop."

"That drop," I answered, "is about nine feet—into water. Why did you stop in the first place?"

"I couldn't have made it to the end," he said.

"I made it in plenty of time." I stopped here because I began to get the idea.

Then I wished I had been the one to think of doing what he had done. Neither of us at that time knew anything about Tom Sawyer, because he was created by Mark Twain instead of Zane Grey, but at least one of us knew how to have an adventure.

The buckeye hunt took place on a pleasant fall day. The reason for collecting buckeyes was never made clear, but we learned a good many things about them. They are large, nutlike seeds related to the horse chestnut. They symbolize Ohio. This always struck me as a strange choice because of all the bountiful and blessed flora grown in the rich soil of Ohio, the buckeye is the least useful—with the possible exception of the spiny nut of the Jimson weed. The buckeye cannot be eaten by man or beast; it is no good as a fertilizer or as building material, nor does it produce a particularly beautiful tree. I suppose, added to a hot enough fire, like a blast furnace, it might make some sort of fuel, but the bother would outweigh the benefit. The real reason for the hunt was an excuse to get outdoors. This was a great idea, except if Mrs. Coon had known what would happen on this trip (which she never did) she might have called it off or at least kept the group closer together.

As soon as we had listened to a chapter of Deuteronomy and the first four chapters of *Riders of the Purple Sage*, we set off down the railroad tracks. It was a warm day. The sun had that mellow paleness that would sharpen into a fierce, white spot in the deep blue of October's sky. But now it was September, and although the weeds were dry, they were not yet crisp. Summer had left neither the leaves nor the air. It was hard to keep from running, so most of us ran. This succeeded in scattering the class. Mrs. Coon must have figured everyone knew the way back, because there was nobody, even in that group, so simple he couldn't follow a railroad track. Among those who did not run were Mrs. Coon and a big kid who joined the Navy the following year and whose name I can't remember. I don't think I really knew it then. He looked to be about her age.

Before long we were making side trips; a few of us had found buckeyes which had to be forced out of their pods.

For awhile I walked with Edna, but when I showed off how I could stay on the rails, jumping from one to another, I forgot about her because Billy was doing the same thing. Presently Edna disappeared with some girls in the woods. After three-quarters of an hour of side trips playing Indian Scout and getting a total of five buckeyes, Billy and I joined Mike Potts who was in a bad mood because he was out of Mailpouch tobacco.

"Wish I had some rope," he said.

"Why?" we asked.

"I'd tie one of you guys to the rail," he said, without grinning. "Good and tight. Stand off in the woods and watch a fast passenger train run over you."

"My brothers'd break your fat neck," Billy said.

"Yeah? Yer brothers 'n what army?"

"Just my brothers."

"Let him alone, Billy," I mumbled. "No sense arguing with him."

"If I tied *him* to the track," Mike said, indicating me, "what's 'at got to do with *your* brothers anyways?"

"'Cause he's a friend of mine, and if he's a friend of mine he's a friend of my brothers, that's what!"

From between the ties Mike had picked up some stones which he now chucked at our feet, trying to make us jump.

"C'mon Mike, quit!" cried Billy. We were moving away from him. We both knew if we turned and ran, he'd aim for our heads, so we increased our speed gradually. When he threw the last stone he had and bent over for more, we plunged down the side of the roadbed and hopped a fence. A few stones came after us, but we were soon halfway across the field. When we looked around, Mike had started back along the railroad.

Since we now found ourselves on the old Clinton place, close to the house and outbuildings, we were going to make a wide circle and come back to the tracks farther west. I stopped and looked at Billy.

"Things seem pretty quiet here," I said. "Too quiet."

Billy stopped walking to look at the buildings, shading his eyes with his hand. "Do you think the Clintons are all right?"

We both knew they were all right, and that they were away visiting their son in Cincinnati. Their grandniece went to school with us.

"They're pretty old, and he's not a good shot at all," I said.

"If any red savages have touched those poor old people—" Billy had a look on his face so grim that I felt a flicker of pity for the red savages.

"You got your powder horn?" he asked. I had. In a moment we had found sticks that served well as rifles and pistols—the kind that bring imaginary frontier characters out of nowhere instead of real squad cars out of police headquarters—and we went toward the house, crouched low. Near one corner of a truck garden we stopped behind a tree. At the other end of the garden was a summer kitchen, joined to the house by a dilapidated porch. We agreed to take opposite sides of this, and scout. Halfway along my side I stopped because I'd heard a sound. A real sound. Something or somebody was inside the summer kitchen. I decided I ought to meet Billy for a counsel, and he must have decided the same thing for the same reason for we met at the rear of the frame building with what must have been the same look on our faces.

"There's somebody in there," he whispered.

"Or some *thing*," I whispered back. "You know, they could have left a door open, and if a grizzly got in, the door could have blown shut. That'd keep him there."

"D'ya s'pose so?"

"Sure. There's no such thing as a grizzly that can work a doorknob. You know that."

"Yeah. But I mean, really. I heard real noises in there."

"So did I. Really. Let's find out what it is if we can, but I don't want to bust in there without a clear path back."

"Let's go get help."

"We don't need any help yet."

"When we do, it might be too late."

"Not if we're careful. But let's stick together. Maybe we can peek in one of the windows."

We got on all fours and crept around the corner. I thought as long as we didn't have help, we ought to be in an upright position, ready to hightail it, but on the other hand it was being more cautious to crawl.

The first window showed us nothing except that the interior of the house was rather dark. But we heard the sounds again—as though someone were having difficulty trying to talk.

It was through the second window that we saw who was there. It was Betty Strunk and Ed Dunlap, and they were half out of their clothes. At first it seemed to me that they'd had an accident or that they'd been fighting and it had come off sort of a draw. They were on an old sofa. Then I realized the truth.

I had known the rudiments of the facts of life ever since I could remember, but few ten-year-olds have access to such visual aids as the demonstration I was now watching. Many people go through long and normal lives without witnessing this process except from the distorted perspective of being involved. Billy and I were at a distance and angle that distorted nothing—and left out no detail.

"What are they doing?" he asked.

"I think it's something you're only s'posed to do if you're married." I whispered this out of the side of my mouth because I couldn't get my head to turn toward him.

"Maybe they're married," Billy said.

I said I doubted it, and after a moment I wanted to quit looking. I felt embarrassed for them and had the idea they ought to be left alone. I also realized that for a big cow, Betty, viewed this way, was a powerfully fascinating big cow.

I finally got Billy away from the window by convincing him Ed would drill us with another twenty-two if he caught us. But for weeks afterward I kicked myself that I had not stayed longer, because I had the feeling I might have missed something. I know now there was very little of an essential nature that I had missed.

"You gonna tell your folks?" Billy asked on the way back.

"I don't know," I said. "I don't see why. I don't see why not either, I guess."

"Is she going to have a baby?" Billy was not totally ignorant.

"Sure she is. But it's none of our business."

Billy chuckled. "Any baby that's ever born is because two people did that?"

"Yeah," I said. "And it isn't easy. Old Betty looked like she was worn out."

Billy shook his head. "I don't see how my parents managed it fourteen times."

We trudged on in the noon of early autumn, each with his own thoughts. The rest of the group had organized and was a little way ahead. When we drew near the cutoff for the school, I said, "That Ed Dunlap is a dirty bum."

"He's a son of a bitch," Billy added.

We felt a little older.

5
If All the World Were Mechanized

I STOPPED AT my end of the wire, frozen. I had suddenly recognized the figure stepping over the ground end of the guy wire that ran thirty feet up to the top of the telegraph pole.

It must have been late afternoon, but I wasn't sure. The light was failing, partly because of a smoky mist that shrouded everything. My knees sagged. I tried to swallow and I felt icy all over. There was no doubt about it—it was Dean. And there was no doubt in my mind that Dean was going to kill me.

Dick Schultz was still at his end of the wire where it was tied to the next pole. He hadn't seen Dean yet. He thought, as I had, that Dean was no longer with us—that he'd been taken away for good. I tried to call to Dick but I couldn't talk and I couldn't move.

I remembered drops of solder on a newspaper lying on the table on the sun porch, and my father building a radio. He put lead foil on the backs of hard rubber panels, wound wire in coils around hard rubber cylinders, and hooked up enormous vacuum tubes to B batteries and A batteries. There were no gang tuning-condensers—he had to set three dials separately—yet squealing sounds came through the headphones and later through the big crinkle-finish horn, shaped like a question mark. KDKA in Pittsburgh, WJW in Detroit and WLW in Cincinnati talked to him, fading in and out, as the voices of gods might have blurred, from sheer majesty and distance.

I could see parts left over—scraps that I had assembled under the table where he worked. I could hear my own voice, changed to sound like those Olympian ones which issued crackling from the big, bent funnel.

I saw vividly the wall outlet, its yawning, threaded socket covered by a round brass lid that you could poke at and lift with a curtain rod if you wanted a bad shock, or a spanking, or both.

"Would you like a real radio on which you and your brother could talk back and forth?" my father had asked.

"Yes!" I cried.

That afternoon he drilled holes in the bottoms of two empty tin cans, then knotted a long wire in two places near the ends, after running it through the cans. Tying the ends so the wire stretched between two telegraph poles in the vacant lot behind Dean Rittenauer's house, he put my brother and me at either end and had one of us talk while the other listened. The vibrations, caught by the diaphragm action of the bottom of one can, were transmitted along the wire and turned into sound again at the other can.

This magic skill surpasses in flavor any revelations I've encountered since. The miracles of Marconi, de Forest, and Zworykin—all are very flat and stale by comparison.

Now my brother had gone in and Dick Schultz, a neighbor boy my age, had taken his place.

It was getting dark. Between us and our homes was Dean Rittenauer, who had said he would kill us if we ever set foot on his lot again. Dean was two years older than Dick and I were, and a lot bigger.

"You thought I wasn't ever comin' back, didn't you?" Dean said, moving closer, his head cocked to one side. "I told you I was goin' to live with my grammaw just to see if you guys'd start walkin' on my land. But I just visited her—whatta you got there?"

"My dad made a radio and we're talkin' on the radio," I stammered.

"Yeah?"

"Yeah. You wanna talk?"

He nodded.

"Hey Dick!" I called. "Talk to him. Let's let Dean talk on the radio! C'mon back!" Dick had edged out to circle around and get to his house after he'd spotted Dean. He hesitated a moment, and then came back.

I told Dean to put his ear to the tin can.

"All right Dick! Say sumpthin'!"

"Sumpthin'!" shouted Dick into the can.

Dean looked up from his end of the apparatus. He had forgotten, at least for the moment, that he was here to kill us.

"Can he hear *me*?"

"Sure. Say sumpthin'!"

"Even if I talk soft?"

"Yeah. My dad built it that way!"

He cleared his throat and looked across at Dick, who still had his ear up close to the can at his end.

"This is the radio man, talking to you through the radio," Dean said softly.

"I heard you! I heard you!" Dick shouted, jumping up and down.

"Yeah, what'd I say?" shouted Dean.

"You said, 'This is the radio man, talking to you through the radio!'"

Dean's wide, freckled face broke into a smile. "Boy, this is okay!" he said.

"You said, 'Boy, this is okay'!" Dick shouted from his end.

"I wasn't even talkin' to him and he heard me!" Dean said, more excited than ever.

"You said, 'I wasn't even talkin' to him and I heard you!' I mean, 'You wasn't even talkin' to you'—oh—you know!"

"Dick Schultz is a nanny goat!" Dean shouted.

"I'm a nanny goat!" Dick cackled. "I heard that two ways! Through the air and over the thing—the radio! Boy!"

I learned something that day—broadcasting, although by no means always employed in the cause, is an instrument of peace.

My father was one of the last to capitulate to an age of specialization. He is the original do-it-yourselfer, and tends to believe that if anything is beyond his powers of comprehension or manipulation, it doesn't really exist. (I say "tends" because he has finally bogged down in toto in dealing with his television set.) I think what discourages the workbench hobbyist, when it comes to highly technical things, is the knowledge that no one person anywhere in the world knows enough to handle certain projects from start to finish. No single human being could assemble an atom bomb or a television set. But TV sets are brought into being from raw materials every day because one team knows how to make special glass for picture tubes and another team knows how to pull the air out of picture tubes and seal them up—and so on down the line.

One drawback in being born into an age of high technology is that we take for granted things that are practically miracles. Dad belongs to the age of transition. Young enough to live among these miracles, he is just old enough to think of them as such. This probably explains his peculiar attitude toward machinery.

Although he has always been extremely long-suffering in his dealings with other humans—he is understanding and able to control his temper remarkably—he could never apply this patience to inanimate things—particularly machines. This is because of a deep and basic suspicion of machinery. The more complex the machine the more hostile Dad is to it. He shares Norbert Wiener's belief that man may be putting himself out on a limb by building machines and letting them take over some of his thinking for him.

In spite of this, he is an inveterate tinkerer, having worked tirelessly on the automation of mechanical things —in effect, teaching them to think. In his own way he was a pioneer—a fact documented by a number of bizarre events.

When we moved to the MacBeth farm, the house was supplied with water from a cistern and a drilled well. In the basement there was a primitive pumping system, supposed to be fed by the cistern. Water was then distributed by a pressure tank through faucets in the kitchen and bathrooms. The equipment was far from perfect. Dad renovated it in a few months' spare time, putting in a new and much more powerful basement pump as well as a larger tank. Since the cistern water was not safe to drink, we pumped well water by hand and kept a tin bucket of it in the kitchen. There was an aluminum dipper in the bucket.

I doubt if I'll ever forget the taste of that water. It was heavy and diamond-clear, and bristling with minerals. It came unendingly, in unchanging character, from some constant source deep in the earth, far removed from the effects of changing seasons, bringing its freshness to fever and dust and sweat. That water gave to memory something silver. And because standards of the taste in water are formed by conditions of youth and thirst, all the water I've tasted since is somehow weak and stale. I've always believed the subject of The Old Oaken Bucket, recruited to serve temperance, is not the moss-covered wooden container with its bright burden, but the author's lost childhood.

Step by step Dad automated our water system until it frightened people. Literally.

When he installed the new house pressure system in the basement, he sealed off the cistern. From here on, as it was all well water, we could drink from the faucets. That system still had its limitations. In those days you couldn't (or at least he didn't) buy a unit that included cutoffs and other control devices. These he built. But again, a step at a time. When the pump was first installed, we had to time its running and shut it off after the pressure had built up to a certain point. Frequently this operation was neglected. Then the loud and agonized clanking of the overburdened pump signaled that the pressure was maybe six or eight times what it ought to be. On these occasions, opening a tap without great caution could mean blasting the dishes out of the sink. Within a single evening a thirsty guest had a glass blown to bits in his hand, while another guest emerged from the bathroom with the lower part of his clothing soaked. He said to Dad, "Very funny, Milton, very funny." And to his wife, "Get your things, Alice, I think we've stayed long enough." The other guests agreed with his first statement, and my parents with his second, so my father nodded pleasantly and showed them to the door.

We still had to supply big drums in the basement with well water from the pump, which was located near the house under an abandoned windmill tower. Dad had run a long pipe from the pump through the foundation into the basement when he sealed off the cistern. Most of the pumping was assigned to Paul and me, but I did my share *and* his. Although I was a little heavier, it took all my weight to bring the cast-iron handle down. At ten, I was not tall enough to operate it properly. With the handle in the Up position, I had to jump up and perch on it like a bantam rooster and bring it to the Down position. These calisthenics produced about a pint of water; the drums were fifty gallons each.

Since Paul was nearly my size he could have taken his turn. I found that out after what seemed like months, but he had proved to Dad that his perching on the handle did nothing but make him look like a hypnotized plover. He couldn't budge the thing. After Dad watched one of these trials I saw Paul remove from the fulcrum a stove bolt which he had put there to block any motion of the handle. I hit him in the eye.

In late summer, 1931, Dad christened a power unit for

the pump made from harrow teeth, binder twine, and machinery rejected by junk yards. It operated roughly on the principle of the internal combustion engine. We called it Milton's Folly, but I cheered it since it represented deliverance from my drudgery.

Dad was getting the hang of control devices. His spare time was largely spent now in refining, and adding to, the concept of work-free living. Some of his effort, however, was spent in what might be called the pursuit of pure science. In the hall between the kitchen and dining room, for example, in an alcove that had had pantry shelves at one time, he had set up a sort of master control panel, on which he tied everything together by elaborate wiring. There were pilot lights, switches, relays, fuses, tubes, rheostats, and some devices I had seen only in movies in the basement laboratories of mad scientists.

At one point there were battery-run emergency lights all over the house for use during power failures, a wind charger with an airplane propeller for keeping the batteries up, a heat-controlled attic fan with louvered vents, a crude stoker that screwed coal out of the coalbin into the furnace, and an electric-eye control on the door from the dining room to the porch (which, never having the proper timing, usually opened on a person's approach in time to catch him square in the face as it swung closed again).

The photo cell fascinated my father. He foresaw many things now in use. "Just think," he'd say, "the photoelectric cell, coupled to a type of rheostat, could make lights come up slowly in your house as daylight faded."

He never got around to that. But he did build an electric timer outlet—a clock that switched appliances on and off at preselected times. It was made with the radio in mind, but we used to plug all sorts of other things into it.

He also rigged a system of closing the windows automatically when rain hit the sill. Although it was impractical to do this all over the house, we had one ground floor window that would close at a drop of rain. My brothers and I nearly wore it out by spitting on the sill.

The turning point was the time of our vacation at a lake in Indiana. We were only gone four days, but none of that family of automatic machines was the same afterward. Dad had hired Mr. Kitchell to stay at the place and look after the stock while we were gone. Kitchell was a seedy old bachelor from nearby Spencerville who had helped on occasion with some of the heavy work. He was stolid and laconic. The little finger of his right hand was missing. He told us that his brother had chopped it off with an ax at his request when he was bitten on it by a poisonous snake years ago in Michigan. I had always thought of him as imperturbable. On our return I was shocked to see him perturbed to a point that might clinically have been described as violent.

It was planned that he sleep in the "office," a small downstairs room that nobody ever used as an office, but which had become a catchall for items of no use but some imagined value. He brought his own Army cot.

On our return, he had his cot in the barn, and he looked fifteen years older. While his account of those four days was not too coherent, we pieced together a general idea of what had happened.

The first night he was awakened by the vacuum cleaner starting up. Someone had left it plugged into the timer. It had taken him awhile to find it and, as he didn't want to get near it, he attacked its cord with a pair of tinsnips. This gave him something of a jolt.

There had been a thunderstorm the second night. At

the first gusts and distant flashes he had tried to close the automatic window, working in vain for several minutes. When he finally gave up and turned his back on it rain started to fall, whereupon the window ground shut by itself, catching part of his nightshirt and holding him prisoner, amid a whir of motor and a ghastly, undulating whine of rack and pinion.

He freed himself after some struggle, and being deathly afraid of the lightning, now flashing jagged bolts followed more and more closely by salvos of thunder, he made his way to the center of the room, away from the windows.

It slowly dawned on him that the house, his refuge from an out of doors saturated with horror, was showing signs of hostility more threatening than the familiar fury of nature. The window biting his nightshirt was only a feeble start.

The lights dimmed, then winked out, due to power failure. Mr. Kitchell was used to this. What he was not used to was the illumination of emergency bulbs in each room—bulbs which had not been in evidence before and for which there were no switches. After a short time, and while he was searching for the fuse boxes, the drain on the batteries activated the release of the fin on the wind charger, which swung into action to bring the batteries back up to full charge. In an ordinary breeze this wind charger made a noticeable racket, and as it was attached to the roof, it sent some vibration through the house. In a full-blown storm the effect was like an airplane readying for takeoff directly overhead, and it was probably heavier than the roof was stressed for.

About the time Mr. Kitchell found the master control panel and discovered the fuses were intact, the power came back, turning on the lights that had been off, while turning off the lights that had been on. However, he had unfortunately fiddled with some of the switches. These switches formed a network of such subtle interrelation and vast complexity that had there been an operating manual (which there wasn't—it was all in Dad's head, which was in Indiana), Mr. Kitchell could not have grasped its rudiments in weeks of study—and at the time he stood there, tiny lamps in the panel winking on and off at him, he must have thought he had only minutes to live anyway.

The havoc he wrought came from throwing perhaps no more than four or five switches. But an inept brain surgeon can work lethal wonders with very little pruning. Having brought his unsterilized hands to the very nerve center of the house, Mr. Kitchell, in a certain sense, deserved his fate.

Suddenly everything leaped into action, for the house, touched to the quick, underwent a paroxysm. The sump pump jumped awake under its hot manhole cover. Louvers opened in the attic wall to let the wind drive the fan blades backwards for a moment, throwing current into the line and shorting the thermostat relays. This switched the fan on and overcame the wind, adding a new vibration.

Mr. Kitchell swore he had heard a toilet flush at the height of all this. It seems unlikely that this was anything but his imagination, although the pressure in the water system was abnormal when we got back.

The stoker came on and ran for two days with no fire in the furnace. The firebox filled with coal, forcing the door open from inside and depositing a half ton of coal at the foot of the furnace and an eighth of an inch of coal dust over every piece of furniture in the house. Mr. Kitchell didn't know this because he didn't go back inside the house after that night.

But he lived up to his agreement and watered the livestock by carrying buckets from the lake.

Dad gave him credit for that, and deep down I think he sympathized with his terror.

"Machines will sometimes turn on you," he said.

6
Chicken à la Downs

IF, IN ADDITION to ingredients and preparation, a television cooking show could get across that final pinnacle of flavor compounded of delay, anticipation, and the innocence of an undefiled palate, it would transcend mere communication. But such is the nature of conveying aesthetic experience that communication serves best when it conveys from one person to another the ability to call up a similar experience. The gap is never truly bridged. Yet I must ask you to do this, and hope that when you were about twelve you had some gustatory experience which you look back on with great fondness; that you can remember some of the aromas across the years. Then only will you fully understand.

The calendar year during which I turned twelve was not a good one for us. The depression was in full swing that year, and in addition to the overall crisis, Dad's business went under. His partner declared separate bankruptcy. Dad could have taken the same course, but instead took a job (which he felt lucky to get) and paid off creditors in full over a long and lean period. The banks had closed the year before.

Dad never wasted emotional energy in expressing (or as far as I knew *feeling*) annoyance. He would not allow himself to feel hounded. He paid when he could, and he refused to feel put upon or guilty when he couldn't. There were unique ways of doing this.

One Sunday morning the whole family had gone to the car, which was kept in a shed about fifty yards from the house. Dad stood aside a moment, looking back toward the road. He had seen a car come up the driveway and guessed correctly that it was a creditor. Since we couldn't get away without driving past the other car, Dad told us to wait where we were until he got rid of the creditor.

He played it by ear. I don't know what he had intended to tell the fellow, but his real opportunity came the instant he moved onto the front porch, and he ad libbed it from there.

"Is the farmer that lives here home?" the creditor asked my father.

"I don't know," Dad said, "I've just been around back. I want to see him, too."

They spent the next few minutes taking turns ringing the doorbell and small-talking the dreariness of being in the collection business. Finally they gave it up, and Dad drove us to church with a clear conscience.

My mother had explained to me, I thought over-seriously, why I would probably never get my money back from the Lima National Trust Company after it folded. She gave a rather beautiful talk about it, detailing the rudiments of economics and enjoining us all to adopt a stoic attitude toward the disaster.

I was able to do this with my hands tied behind me because the total amount I lost was twelve dollars, which I never expected to see again anyway. I knew that ultimately it would have been withdrawn to buy school supplies or clothing or some other foolishness, which was only fair since the money had not been put there by me. If it had been mine it would never have been deposited to begin with—it would have been spent.

During those lean years we ate hundreds of chickens. We raised them to sell, but no one could afford to buy them. Quite a variety of dishes derived from this source—we had chicken broiled, stewed, fried, roasted, braised, fricasseed, southern style, à la King, chicken Tetrazzini, cacciatore, Jeannette, Quebec, Biarritz, Yorkshire, down East, paprika, Mornay, paella and Berryman. (This last was a family joke —a term for overdone chicken, named for a neighbor, Angus Berryman, who burned down his house for the insurance.) We had giblet hash, wing-bone soup, croquettes, pies, chopped chicken liver, chicken sandwiches, chicken salad, chicken salad sandwiches, cockerel casserole and Plymouth Rock pot luck.

There was a veal imitation of chicken available in markets. They'd sell artificial chicken legs made of veal, ground and treated in some way and wrapped around sucker sticks. One day my youngest brother Wallace, then six, asked for some of these. He said he'd always liked them. To my mother's credit, instead of laughing at him or hitting him, she took sticks from an old clothes rack, trimmed them to the right size, and pressed around these an artificial ground veal which she made of chicken leftovers. They were delicious, and I'm not sure it was ever clear to Wally that his veal imitation of chicken was really a chicken imitation of a veal imitation of chicken.

Anyway, back to the ambrosial plate I spoke of earlier, curvetting yet through a corridor of nostalgia to haunt my jaded taste buds. Somewhere I had read of an old Roman method of cooking chicken. I wanted to try it. Preparing the fowl called for cleaning it inside, but leaving its feathers on, then covering it completely with a thick wall of mud.

The whole thing was then to be deposited in a pit one-third full of hot coals, covered with dirt taken from the pit, and baked in its mud cocoon for three hours.

On a Sunday night in July, Paul and I catered what today would be called a cookout. The whole family feasted royally in the orchard.

Mom made potato salad and took care of such other details as cucumbers, olives, lemonade, coffee, cake and watermelon. She also lugged everything out and back and washed up afterwards, and headed a committee of thanks from the rest of the family for the marvelous meal my brother and I fixed all by ourselves.

About midafternoon Paul and I took off with spades for the Black Forest, our name for a grove on the other side of the orchard, to dig the pit. Inside the orchard was a line of Catalpa trees whose pods would not crack until later on toward fall. Moving into the forest itself, in summer, one was astonished to find the grovelike character quickly changing, as the path led downward into a heavy gloom that was forbidding. Thin, round grass stems gave way, as the trees came closer and bigger, to undergrowth, and then to a floor of leaves long dead. The elm trunks, at first shaggy and small, and interspersed with mulberry, finally shared space with thick-boled pines. Overhead the light was almost shut out, in some places no sky was visible, and the clay floor in the lowest places had a bluish cast where it wasn't deep with needles. Heavy vines writhed up the sides of the tunnel that made the path. Occasionally pockets of mist hung across the way as if barring intruders. The Shawnees, we had always believed, considered the mists to be poison. We were certain the Shawnees still lived somewhere farther along the path, beyond our farthest point of penetration.

After we'd picked a spot well into the grove and turned the first earth, Wally brought us word that we were to come back and change our clothes "this instant." Since he carried some of the same inflection with which these instructions must have been given to him by Mom, we blamed him for the annoyance.

"Why?" Paul asked.

"Because those are the clothes you went to church in," Wally told him.

"We're not gettin' 'em dirty. All we're doin' is diggin' a pit."

"What for?"

I could tell, somehow, in that split second of silence that followed, exactly what was going to happen.

"We —" Paul started haltingly, "we weren't s'posed to tell you right now, but you may as well know."

"Know what?" Wally's six-year-old innocence must have been pathetic, standing there as he was with his little smiling face—but at the time he was merely, once again, the target for the incredible cruelty of older brothers.

"We're diggin' it for you," I said softly.

"It's your final resting place," Paul added. There was a catch in his voice and he wiped his eye on his sleeve. He was overdoing it.

"Yeah?" Wally asked, still smiling. "Why?"

"You went one step too far." I sank the spade again, shaking my head slowly. "Remember yesterday when you planed off the corners of the front porch? That was the automatic death sentence. Dad didn't have the heart to do the job himself so he told us to."

"Soon's we get this dug we have to load the shotgun."

Wally stopped smiling.

"You stand at one end and we blindfold you with a

handkerchief and when we fire you fall in and then we fill 'er back up."

"That's why we're wearin' our church clothes," Paul said.

Wally backed two steps, his chin quivering, then turned and leaped into a sizzling sprint for the house, baying butchery in a sustained and hysterical blast which shattered the Sabbath stillness. He knew perfectly well we didn't really mean what we said. At any rate, the prank wasn't traumatic. Next day he was lying in wait for us with a pail of scrubbing water which he administered from the porch roof with the skill and dispatch of a boy twice his age.

We made two errors in our preparations of that meal which canceled each other neatly. First, we started a wood fire in the pit and then added coal from the basement. We kept adding all afternoon. Soon it was impossible to get within ten feet of it without singeing our eyebrows. It was level to its brim with glowing coals. Second, it was 5:30, and the chickens had yet to go into the pit. To wait the three hours for 8:30 would have mangled my father's amiability badly, and the family would have suffered more than hunger. As it was, by 7:00 o'clock we were bolstering his wilting patience with funny jokes and interjections of "Any minute now!" and "Just a *lit-tle* longer, and *boy!*", or sometimes (although it didn't produce the calculated effect), "Boy, wait till you taste this!" This last naturally inspired the acid observation that he *was* waiting, so we'd go back to funny stories which brought weaker and more hollow laughter as the sun moved down over the lake in the northwest.

We had mudded the chickens about 4:30 and got them good and heavy with alternate layers of yellow clay, gray clay and brown mill-bottom loam. As it became apparent that the fire was much hotter than we felt it ought to be, built as it was of almost half a winter's supply of coal, we were afraid to drop our chickens into it. So we kept adding layers of mud in the hope that this protection would offset the intensity of the fire.

It was all we could do to lift them. Finally we rolled them into the coals and threw the dirt over them, at first from a distance and then closer until all the sod was replaced. By that time we had created a smoking mound that would have startled a passer-by with its similarity to a nascent volcano.

Dad walked into the Black Forest at last, although we had asked him not to, and viewed the pit with less than happy anticipation. I'd have called it despair.

"They're in there?" he asked, pointing.

"What?" I asked.

"The chickens. They're in there?"

"Yes. And any minute now —"

"Why does it steam like that?"

"I suppose that's the water in the mud," Paul said.

Dad looked at us heavily.

"You're in league with the devil," he said, and went back to the orchard to brood and pick some more at the food already spread and waiting. When the chickens were at last ready the pickles and bread were gone. This was at 7:30, or a little after, and they'd been in the pit about two hours.

We pushed the dirt aside, and with a long-handled shovel I got under one misshapen clay lump and moved it out just before the steel in the shovel blade was ready to melt.

Each clay ball had shrunk slightly and was black in places. Tapping it with a shovel showed that it was now a brick. I swatted one of them several times with a spade. Paul ran to the barn for an ax. On his second blow it cracked. Steam came out with some pressure behind it. We looked at each other.

"That's how diamonds are formed," Paul said. "There may be nothing in there but a big diamond."

"You call that nothing?" I asked him. "I'll take that kind of nothing any day in the week. Boy!"

"It'd have to be awful big, as hungry as Dad is."

The clay shell had cracked wide open now. Using forks and pot holders, we got the first skinned chicken onto the platter. It was not burned, it was not underdone. It was just right.

With only the addition of salt, we had chicken as delicious as any I've ever tasted or imagined. To give full scope to the rhapsody would verge on sensuality. It was, let me say simply, yummy.

The family was lavish in its praise. Paul and I strutted a little. Although there was no bread left to go with it, we made up for this in potato salad. The feast was a success.

Dad's mood lifted like a great fog on a mountaintop departing in majesty and letting the last long rays of the sun smile through. By the time night had made silhouettes of trees and buildings he was positively jovial. Even the insects—at first gnats, and then mosquitoes—which finally closed in good, amused rather than annoyed him.

Before returning to the house we all went to look at the pit. It glowed at us pleasantly as we ringed it not far from the edge. The night air was cool; the warmth of the coals felt good.

"A tremendous fire like this for just one meal," Dad said, shaking his head. "Too bad we can't do this again."

"Do you mean now?" Mother asked.

"No. I meant tomorrow and perhaps Tuesday and Wednesday. I can't imagine this going out right away."

"It won't," Paul said brightly. "We put a lot of coal on it." I winced in the dim light.

Dad said, "Yes, I know you did. If we run out of coal next winter we can all come out here with blankets and sleep as near your pit as the heat will let us." He chuckled. "This will probably burn till business gets better."

We stood there a moment and then started back through the trees to the house, each filled with that real wealth the wealthy often counterfeit—solid contentment.

7
Talent, Tenacity and Trowels

EVERY LIVING creature has a driving force that pushes him in the direction of certain goals. Some creatures, and some human beings, appear to have more of such a force than others. But in no single individual is it operative at its peak all the time. While there may seem to be a connection between strength of driving force and goal, this is not always rational or even discernible.

For example, before getting into broadcasting, I displayed no driving force in finding a job. But after one whiff of the broadcast business (a business thoroughly impractical, and for which I had no reason to think I was particularly equipped, having not one shred of background, and not one trouper in the family), my driving force pranced blindly out of its stall snorting fire, determined to carry me to success. I didn't just want to be a broadcaster—I wanted to broadcast. And this in the face of palpable terror. Like Joan of Arc, who loathed soldiery, but took it up as a necessary tool of an obsessive wish, I faced without relish the mike fright, the weird hours, the loss of anonymity (which like virginity, once lost is not to be regained), the head-shaking of my relatives and counselors (who "had thought he was a more stable lad than that—his family certainly tried to bring him up with a sense of values!"), the almost incredible pay (a boy who ran a downtown newsstand netted exactly twice as much as I did per week), the drudgery of small-station chores which are not glamorous—schedule and log, record filing, setup, sweep-out—all these things I faced, I say without cheer, but dismissed them as a paltry price for my burning ambition. And what precisely was the goal of that ambition? Fame? Attention? It didn't fit with the deep dread of simply being heard by people who tuned in on their radios. Money? Ultimate material gain? Vast holdings and temporal power? I don't believe I thought for an instant that there was a remote chance of it, and I don't believe I sought it. A great need to get to the populace with what I believed to be The Message? Hardly. I not only had nothing to say, I would be lucky if I could get through a commercial for the local feed store without fainting. I had no urgent tidings to impart, no political opinions, no philosophy, and scarcely any specific ambition within the framework of the profession. It was as if I were called for reasons to be divulged to me later. But without consciousness of any such reasons, the desire to broadcast was very real. I would be content at first to follow convention to the letter—to read what others had written, to shun innovations, so long as I was broadcasting.

The beauty of a driving force is that, blind as it may be, it differs from a mere impetus in that it doesn't just give you a push—it keeps propelling you. Tenacity is an important characteristic of the true driving force. Again, mysteriously, reasons for tenacity may be lacking, but when it's there it's there. It is sometimes called stubbornness. I have had it at times, and it is absent from my actions at times.

But I remember once . . .

The transition from MacBeth School to Shawnee Centralized was accompanied by some new clothes to replace what I'd outgrown, which was everything, and this new apparel included a man-style overcoat and a felt hat. My brother Paul entered the part of the fifth grade that I had skipped altogether, while Jim started in the first.

I cut quite a figure on the junior high bus. By the middle of the first semester I was trying to force my voice to change by growling low whenever I was alone, until I developed real pain just behind my Adam's-apple. I also knew all the words to "We Just Couldn't Say Good-by," and did a fair imitation of Joe Penner.

One of the required courses in the seventh grade was manual training. It exposed my lack of handiness rather painfully. I passed it, squeakily, through the careful choice of projects and help obtained by the scurviest means. I would, for example, gouge myself slightly with a sharp chisel and then go over and offer to help some skilled lad who didn't need help, and manage to bleed on his work. In my fever to be of service to him, I would wave away the injury as nothing. Naturally he would reward such devotion by reciprocating and bringing to bear on my project all the polish of his innate craftsmanship.

I was not always so coldly calculating, however, and often felt bitter that I was not endowed with more simple dexterity. Out of this bitterness, perhaps, came the first real flair of tenacity I can remember showing.

TALENT, TENACITY AND TROWELS

Determined on this occasion to do something right and without help, I made up my mind to see a shop project through if it killed me.

It nearly did.

We were all making garden trowels out of sheet metal and flat iron bars riveted together in two places. I had had some trouble with the blade part, which was cut out of sheet metal with heavy shears. For awhile it threatened to look more like a giant mechanical moth than a trowel, but I kept trimming it down until it was the right size, though lopsided, and then I trimmed away at it some more until Mr. Woodburn thought I was forging a bayonet; but he thought it would do all right for planting small bulbs. It was the handle that really raised hell.

I stayed after school by myself one day, which was all right with the faculty as long as the power tools were locked up. All I had to do was cut a length of flat iron strip, drill two holes in it and in my sheet metal blade, bend the iron around into an eyelet, pitching it slightly to form the handle shape, then rivet the two pieces together.

Without knowing it I selected a strip of highly tempered spring steel, which couldn't be worked unless it was white-hot and for which King Arthur would have traded his sword Excalibur. It was three-quarters of an inch wide and three-eighths thick, but it took a little over two hours and nine hack saw blades to cut through it. By the time I tried to bend it I was convinced I was a weakling, because everyone else in the class had accomplished this operation with their soft iron in about a half hour, rivets and all.

It would bend slightly in the vise, but return instantly to its original straightness.

I remember saying out loud, "Well sir, we'll just see who's boss here, you or me!" and then going kind of berserk. I somehow moved the big anvil into a position that allowed me to clamp tong handles into a bench vise nearby, and taking up a twenty-five-pound sledge, I flailed away at my steel until I was wringing wet. When I missed once, coming down with the wood handle of the sledge on the anvil, I thought I'd broken both hands. I did crack the hammer handle. In the end the only undamaged article in the room was my trowel handle. It was still straight and looked as though it had just come out of a glass case at the Bureau of Standards.

I decided then and there to make a trowel with a straight handle. A trowel with a straight handle that looked like a bayonet. Individuality is prized in this country, and properly.

I took all the temper out of five drill bits and broke three before I got two holes through that piece of Damascus. The riveting was simple.

Suddenly I was finished. It was dark outside, but I basked in a glow of pride. I had stuck to it, and the world was richer by one trowel. There probably isn't another garden trowel in the universe that has a handle of case-hardened, high-carbon vanadium tool steel, but my father has one in his basement to this day. Mother used it for planting small bulbs.

The next morning I was asked to go to the principal's office. As I approached I heard him talking with Mr. Woodburn. "Yes," he was saying, "but how could he ruin an *anvil?*"

I thought I saw a gleam of admiration in his eye. "You don't look like much, but I guess you're wiry, eh?" He slapped me across the back and laughed, and said something about the football team. Then he asked me to be more careful when I worked in the shop—there were others to consider; those tools and materials belonged to all of us, after all, and so forth. I told him I'd watch it from here on.

8

Stage Fright: Innocence or Arrogance?

TWENTY-ONE years have passed since I sat in a small control room, green-faced and palsied, a salt shaker microphone hanging ten inches in front of me. I had just made my first commercial announcement on the air, and another was due in ten minutes. The program director of the one-hundred watt station stood behind me. He chuckled and said, "A year from now you'll look back and laugh."

"A year from now," I croaked, "I'll be dead."

People often feel fear when thrust into the glare of public attention. It is variously known as stage fright, mike fright, and camera shyness. It is totally unknown to some folks and quite pronounced in others.

My father, a man of intuitive wisdom, pegs stage fright as arrogance rather than humility, pointing out that the discomfort of the frightened performer is rooted in his delusion that what he is doing is of such cosmic importance that the earth might stop turning if he goofed. The truth is that his audience, barring nervous relatives, doesn't give much of a damn how he comes off and is mostly only concerned that he doesn't take too long with it.

This view is not only wise on my father's part, it is brave, because he suffers worse from stage fright than anyone I've ever known. Perhaps twice in his life he has had to address throngs of eight or ten people and has avoided fainting only by remaining seated. I am sure if he found himself substituting for Clyde Beatty in a cage of lions in the center ring, he would turn his back on the cats and aim his whip and chair at the audience.

So in analyzing stage fright the way he does, he admits he is arrogant, which is a truly humble thing to do, and certainly confusing to anyone trying to figure out my father.

Anyway, part of my getting used to being on the air, and part of the reason I stayed alive those first few days, was the application of his theory, which brought the comforting knowledge that everyone has a dial on his radio, and if he doesn't care for me and what I am saying, all he has to do is switch to another station. There is no captive audience in broadcasting. To this day I occasionally feel slightly nervous before getting into certain broadcast bits, but only when a specific person or group is known to be tuned in for a particular reason, where my kicking it might cause harm or embarrassment. But the millions of free and casual viewers and listeners are like millions of friends who are close enough to be comfortable with—tolerating any reasonable thing you do, and capable of leaving you suddenly without making a big thing of it.

I once interviewed a policeman who had been in a gun fight with a desperate killer and had come through it unscathed. After the broadcast he told me he had been much more afraid of the microphone than he had been of the killer. I said that the reverse would be true with me, if I ever faced a situation like that, adding that my fear was probably more rational (to whatever extent fear is rational) since a microphone cannot endanger one's life and a killer can. He agreed, but said it wouldn't help him if he had another broadcast to go through.

The first college-level observations on fear that were aimed my way, along with observations on many other subjects, came from a lad named Harold Liggett, with whom I once worked in a tire warehouse, back in Lima.

I helped hoist incoming shipments of tires to the loading dock and stacked them in a vast storage room where they waited to be put on trucks for distribution to dealers in twenty counties. Lig was unable even to simulate industry. His philosophy was carefully thought out and endless, and bore no relation whatever to his actions or real attitudes.

"You've gotta look busy even if you aren't," he'd tell me. "If you've done all you can for the boss—not only what you're supposed to, but extra stuff above and beyond the call of duty, and there's just nothing more to do, stay out of sight. Avoid the appearance of idleness. Sloth, we call it in college."

I learned things from Lig's conversations, and I learned never to imitate his behavior on the job. In spite of his advice, Lig would rush to and from the railroad station on an assignment, re-enter the front office, and in full view of his employer, seat himself in an upholstered chair with his feet on the desk and leaf through magazines from the stack placed there for waiting service customers.

One night Lig and I had to work well past closing time, stacking tires. As he had a key, we agreed it would be better to eat something, then come back to finish. "Because," he said, "driving yourself without food is ostentatious asceticism which, you'll learn when you get to college, is showing off how you can rise above your appetite. You should always rise above your appetites without any fanfare." His tone carried the conviction that he possessed the ability to soar above his personal desires without a ruffle or a flourish, where the fact was Lig was positively mired in his appetites and was very loud about it. His recounting of conquests involving girls he and I both knew (which contradicted his stated code of a gentleman's behavior in these matters) was motivated by the noble wish to smooth the path for a younger friend.

On this night we had eaten at an Italian restaurant. All through the meal and afterward during the tire-stacking, Lig held forth eloquently on an impressive range of subjects. I had never realized in what neat packages colleges were capable of dispensing Ultimate Truth. At the time, the clarity and impact of his reasoning even dimmed in my mind the question why older people who had been to college and had had years of practical experience didn't have the certainty about things which Lig had as a sophomore.

He spoke of responsibility, self-interest, old age, socialism, sex, stoicism, fear and fearlessness, and economics—not in that order. Sex was last. Sex was always the last topic, even if first, for then it was the only one. His thoughts on fear were brilliant, with the academic solidness of never having been sullied by practical application. Although Franklin D. Roosevelt had not yet made his comment on the nature of fear, Lig's dissertation anticipated it as I remember.

"The reasoning process can do away with fear," he said, "replace it with intelligent concern. Fear is a blind instinct. It had its uses when we were apes, but after the old brain was installed, there was no need. A lot of instincts become useless. Useless appendages is the technical term."

Lig was kind enough always to give me the simple, down to earth explanation along with the college terminology. I found early that he did better in stating his views if I didn't interrupt with questions about opposing ideas. So I rarely did, unless something called for clarification by knocking down a possible objection. I felt this way about fear being a useless appendage.

"Aren't there things we run into that we're better off being afraid of?" I asked him as we alternated swinging a load of truck tires onto a rising stack.

"Like what?"

"Well, like if you were sleepy and some danger showed up, being afraid will make you pretty wide-awake and ready for action."

"You think that's good?" Lig leaned on one of his tires.

"Well, if I had to take some fast action, I'd rather be wide-awake than stay sleepy and blasé, and maybe throw away my chances—maybe my life." Blasé was a word I'd heard him use.

"You've got a point, boy, but you're missing the boat." He paused, as though considering how to simplify the presentation of his restatement without making it sound too patronizing.

"When I say intelligent concern I mean alertness and fast employment of the old bean without the kind of worry that hurts you—hurts your ability to act the best way—to take the best action."

"I think I see. But the alertness might never—"

"You see, it's like an explosion." He handed me one of his tires to hoist. "Blind fear is a lot of energy going off in all directions, and though it's designed to blow up the danger it's just as apt to blow you up along with it.

Whereas intelligent concern is like a controlled explosion like you have in a gun. There the explosion is harnessed and directed toward the target—danger. You see?"

That made sense but it didn't answer my question.

"What about laying your hand on a hot steam pipe?" I asked. "You don't have to think 'My hand is on a hot steam pipe; I should take it away before it fries.' You yank it away long before intelligent concern—"

"Wait a minute," he said, "You're talking now about reflexes." I knew I was in a corner. I got along better with Lig as a pupil than as a debating opponent, and besides he was right about this.

"Reflexes happen too fast to involve an emotion like fear. Fear gets you all keyed up for action, but then it can keep you from taking the right action—the action your gray matter figures out for you. Since there isn't any intelligence in fear itself, it has to be kept in control by the mind. Shackled by the mind is one of the college ways of saying it. You'll learn that if you take psych."

I had all my tires up at this point. We had divided them equally before starting to stack. Lig methodically took half his tires and gave them to me. We continued to alternate.

"Another thing," he continued, "fear has no sense of proportion. Can't we start a new pile? This one's getting too high to lift these things."

"I guess we better."

"That's using the old noodle." He laid one of his tires down as a base and I put one of mine on top of it.

"The child," he went on, "is often afraid of things he doesn't have to be afraid of, and fearless about really dangerous things. Part of growing up is learning what to be careful about and what is unimportant. For example, a kid will run across the street without looking, but he won't go in his room with the light out. Doesn't make sense. When he grows up he thinks things out and overcomes the senseless fears. At the same time developing a healthy respect for cars. You follow?"

I did. I also stacked. Having warmed to his task of edifying, he doubtless felt justified in letting me do the manual labor. I was vicariously working my way through college. Besides, grunting under a truck tire robbed his disquisition of the dignity required for being forceful.

We finally finished. By then the talk had turned to sex. The bridge was from inner tubes to Fallopian tubes; once crossed, it set us into that billion-faceted land from which no adolescent traveler returns until the next day. Lig knew a lot about sex, having taken some pre-med courses incidental to his major, which was business administration. He also boasted of his prowess with a keenness of detail that formed a suspicious silhouette against his repeated statement that those who talk the most about it do the least of it.

We had switched off the warehouse lights and were standing in a small office near the stairs. The one remaining light cast long shadows as it ebbed to blackness down the dark corridors between pillars of tires. In those days there were over a dozen different sizes of automobile tires, besides tires for trucks, tractors, airplanes, earth movers, and special industrial vehicles. There is something organic about tires, over and above the fact that they are made mostly of an organic substance—the smell of dusty rubber in large quantities; the way a tire dries out and rots from disuse. The long, gloomy rows of stacked vehicle shoes that disappeared in darkness made us feel less alone and more alone at the same time. We began talking in lower tones now that the place was not so brightly illuminated.

Lig took a long drag on a cigarette. "Take Ethel," he was saying. "She's twenty-six. Probably won't let a man touch her. Sits in that front office five and a half days out of the week punching that adding machine, just dying for it and doesn't even know what's wrong with her."

Ethel had a good figure but little in the way of facial beauty. I had never bothered to think of her problems.

"Best thing in the world for her," Lig said, "would be if we could have her here right now . . . you, and me, and Ethel . . ."

I chuckled. Partly because the vision of Ethel in that little upstairs office with neither her adding machine nor her clothes was incongruous, and partly out of satisfaction that Lig had included me in the role of potential benefactor to girls in need.

He grinned. "Can't you see her? Struggling a little, but not too much, and saying, 'Now you boys stop that!' and all the time scared we might!" He puffed vigorously on his cigarette and his eyes flashed. "Hey, maybe next time we get a shipment we ought to plan to load it in at night and ask her if she'd come back after hours to help us with the count." He was perspiring.

There was something about the way he said it that made me realize he was serious.

"I don't know." I started. Then, realizing I might be sounding like a wet blanket, "It'd sure be a lot of fun. But it'd be fierce if it ever got out. Which one of us would have to marry her if she got—" I was interrupted by two simultaneous things—Lig's clutch on my arm, and a prolonged and heavy sound at the rear of the warehouse—tires, dozens of them, tumbling to the floor.

Mr. Richards had told me during my first week there that sometimes a stack of tires, piled unevenly, will slowly compress on the leaning side, shifting the center of gravity until finally it topples over. Sometimes it will strike other stacks on its way down and they strike still others in a chain reaction that can make a mess of a large inventory.

Lig tightened his grip on my arm until the noise stopped.

The hair on the back of my neck rose. My immediate conclusion, even while I was remembering Mr. Richard's explanation, was that some prowler, tiptoeing to the office to rob it, had pushed over a stack of tires. I only hoped I could master my fear enough to act in the way Lig had prescribed—with intelligent concern. I had the concern, right at the outset and that was half the battle. Now I looked to him to set the pattern.

The pattern he set was very complicated. His intelligence must have been functioning, for he asked in a husky whisper if I thought they kept a gun in the roll-top desk in that office. When I said no, he showed further intelligence by not taking my word for it. He rushed to the desk and flinging up its slatted top, he ransacked it with astonishing thoroughness and speed. I went over to him.

"I think the tires fell over by themselves," I whispered.

"How many steps is it to the door?" he rasped.

"What do you mean?"

"To the top of the stairs!" His eyes were bulging.

"Only about five."

"Gotta keep calm," he whispered. "Jesus!" He crouched. "We'd never make it! Who's got a key? Who'd sneak in and hide? Maybe a joke. One of the boys—"

"Maybe it's Ethel. You said she's love-starved. If she knew we were here—"

"Can you get out there and turn on a light? That might stop him long enough for us to get started down the stairs." He stopped, panting.

I suppose in fairness to him I should point out that he had become pretty excited talking about Ethel, and a powerful emotion like that could easily be converted into another one under the proper circumstances. I didn't feel like reminding him that fear was a useless appendage, since I couldn't have done it without sounding sarcastic. Besides, I wasn't too calm myself. I didn't feel like going out into the warehouse to switch on a light, either.

"Let's just go to the stairs and down. It's not far."

He stood up. "That's using the old noggin," he said. "I wanted to see how you'd react." He faced the door, clenched his hands and then relaxed them. "O.K. Let's go."

We went out. A little light from the night sky came through a window and showed up the doorway at the top of the steps. I led the way.

Lig's first two or three steps were as orderly as you could want. Then he broke into a blind run, brushing heavily against me as he passed. He slammed into the doorjamb and for a second was grotesquely silhouetted against the window with an upflung arm. Then he headed into the stairs. Fortunately, the staircase was a closed affair with wooden walls, or he'd have gone over the side for sure. As it was, I could hear him ricocheting off the walls in a manner that convinced me he was not always on his feet. He certainly wasn't when he reached the bottom, where I found him on the cement floor. When I got the light on and the place seemed less of a nightmare, he was coming to.

"I think I lost my matches," he said, patting his pockets and taking out a cigarette. "No, here they are. Take my advice, boy, don't trip on that top step like I just did."

"You took a real header. You okay?"

"Ha. Don't worry about me. It's late. Let's get out of here." He looked up the steps into the dark. Then he stood up stiffly and limped a step. "Boy!" he said. "Tried to kill myself. Let's go."

I couldn't think of anything to say, and I felt awkward about helping him.

Out on the street he said, "You think they went over by themselves? The tires?"

"I think so."

He took out his handkerchief and wiped some blood from above his right ear. "It's a matter of balance. Equilibrium, we call it in college. See you tomorrow."

"Good night, Lig. You better put some iodine on that."

We walked away, each in his own direction. Half a block away he called to me. "We oughta get Ethel up there, no kidding. In the daytime!"

9
TV Technique — the Unknown Quantity

Knowledge of how much and what kind of impact a communications medium has on the public is essential to the development of a technique for that medium.

My fifth grade teacher, Mrs. Coon, once questioned us about the pronunciation of the word "inquiry." She spelled it for us and asked, "How do you pronounce it?"

Most of us had never heard of it. We guessed at it. Then she asked Jim Stevens to look it up in the big unabridged dictionary on a lectern in the corner.

"It's in-*quire*-ee," he announced at length.

"That is wrong!" beamed Mrs. Coon. We should have been shocked, I suppose, at her finding the dictionary wrong, and wondered at her having tapped a source that let her spot an error in the Ultimate Book of Pronunciations. We merely waited, however, because we were fifth-graders.

"It's wrong," she explained, "because I heard it on the radio last night, and it's *in*-query." We were willing to accept this, but she went on. "That dictionary was copyrighted in 1925, and it was last night I heard it on the radio." That settled it. "The broadcast," she clinched her argument, "was last night, and the dictionary is six years old."

In later years I was to learn the fallacy of her misplaced faith. She could have been listening to an announcer who didn't know how to pronounce his own name, let alone cross swords with Noah Webster. But because she had heard it "on the radio," it blasted the printed word right off the page.

One of the best announcers I know, Norman Barry of NBC Chicago, tells me that when he first auditioned at NBC, Bill Hay was head of announcers there. Readers old enough to remember the original "Amos 'n Andy" broadcasts will recall the announcer who ended the lead-in to each episode with "Here they are!" That was Bill Hay.

When Barry met him, and told him he wanted to audition for a staff position, Hay asked him again for his name.

"Norman Barry," Norm said, pronouncing it like "berry."

"Is that B-e-double-r-y?" asked Hay.

"No. It's B-a-double-r-y," Norm explained.

"Then it's pronounced Barry (baa-ree), not Berry (bear-ee)," said Hay brusquely. "Come back when you can pronounce your own name."

The fact that Barry is a much better announcer than Hay ever was does not erase the fact that Hay was right, and it shows the extent of possible error in broadcast pronunciations.

Although speech consciousness and language aptitude are to be found in above average degree in my family, I am not heavily endowed with either. I remember being derisive of my mother's pronunciation of the word "half" when I was little. She gave the *a* a softened broadness which was a beautiful compromise between the British "hahf" and colloquial Ohio's rather shallow "haff"—in some cases "heh-yuff"—and I accused her of being affected. She tolerated my attitude and patiently fed me, by hand, a sense of correct speech, while I bit the hand.

I took a public speaking course when I was in my junior year at Shawnee which did a lot to arrange and clarify my approach to communication in all its forms. But it could hardly be said to have steered me into broadcasting. The teacher was a remarkable fellow whose stated ambition was to be kicked out of the public school system. He accomplished this without any cheap trickery like making passes at the principal's wife, but simply by delivering a series of minor shocks to the crystallized outlook of schooldom.

For example, he taught what he believed in and spoke freely about it; I learned in that eleventh grade classroom that censure can be earned without holding censurable views. It can be caused by voicing views endorsed by orthodoxy, but which orthodoxy feels should remain unvoiced. Nothing this man said publicly was censurable—only the fact that he said it. In this public speaking class he would encourage discussions on subjects ranging from euthanasia (which he was against) to church architecture (which he wasn't against) and pupils quoting him fairly could not have carried home any material or slant fit to cause an emergency meeting of the board. But there was such a meeting and he was bounced, and I suspect an honest statement of the charge against him would be that he incited his students to think.

Jerry Griffith believed that public speaking should not be approached through speechmaking, but through polishing one's skill in communciation of ideas to other individuals, then to small groups, and finally to large groups, keeping the same informality, and above all keeping the sense of proportion that makes protocol serve communication and not the other way around. Hence the class discussions.

He would take shy kids who couldn't speak their names to more than four people without choking. Soon he would have them voicing earnest opinion to the whole class without knowing they were giving a speech.

"You shouldn't be giving a speech," he would say, "or you shouldn't be on the radio unless you have something to say. If you have something to say, say it and forget about making a speech."

Several times we were required to prepare something, then stand squarely in front of the class and deliver it. I never finished one of these formal talks. He would always say, when I had progressed a few lines into it, "Sit down, Downs. You don't know what you're talking about, and we can't waste time." In spite of this I got good grades. I asked him about it.

"You like to talk," he said bluntly, "and when you like something, you tend to do it fairly well. It would be a waste of time for the class to listen to you—not to what you might have to say, but to your saying it. I grade you on other things."

One day a State Supervisor of Something-or-other was visiting the classes in Shawnee. Jerry waited till the man got to our room, then curled up in the window and directed Jack Peterson to take over the class.

Jack ran things smoothly. At one point in a discussion that developed, a girl asked Jerry's opinion about Plato's old-age longing for the quiet orthodoxy of Egypt. From his window sill seat our teacher gave an opinion. Thereupon two of us who disagreed with him talked him down. The State Supervisor was plainly shocked.

It was one of the most enlightening courses I ever took, and it was the last year he taught.

What is correct speech? If we say it is speech that will not arouse scorn or laughter, then we should have different standards for it in Boston and in Pine Bluff, Arkansas. If you travel, and would avoid giving offense or being laughed at, you would need a high skill in dialect that should cause the Beacon Hill resident to entertain no doubt that you are a Bostonian, the Pine Bluffer to believe you spent your best years in the Ozarks. This theory, to be watertight, is not only very demanding, it is impossible. Because someday you'll find yourself with the Pine Bluffer and the Bostonian during the same conversation.

This is the case in broadcasting, except that you have conversations where you do all the talking, not only to these two citizens simultaneously, but to San Diegans, Poughkeepsians, Wheelingers, Walla Wallans and Miamese. How do you choose a dialect acceptable to them all? Is there such a thing?

There is. Not all broadcasters have it. Ben Grauer, one of the best announcers of all time, gives away the fact that he grew up in the East every time he opens his mouth. I could not hide the flavor of a midwestern background if I wanted to. I don't.

One escape is to become a character and slop on the colloquial characteristics with a wide trowel. This is often done with great success. If you are British and know you could never fool Americans about it, and happen to be an actor or an author, then it would be folly to adulterate your mother tongue. What you must do is accentuate it to a point where you are scarcely understandable, and you will be loved. If you are from Indiana, apply the same technique; with any talent to support it you can become a Herb Shriner. But is there a dialect that is no dialect? A speech pattern acceptable to and (more important) *unnoticed* by all regions? Is there a "correct" speech in this sense?

Dave Garroway's speech is about as close to it as you can get, probably because he speaks an unlumpy blend of dialects from all parts of the country. He says he went to thirteen different schools in thirteen cities before he got to high school. And most of his audience is willing to believe he might have come from their particular part of the country.

Texts on the subject list requirements and qualifications for broadcasting in radio and television, and many claim to teach these. Correct speech is one of many such requisites. It is not the most important. Other qualities show up in these lists—voice-timbre, appearance, presence, sincerity, warmth, nimbleness of mind, and others.

Many immeasurable and some indefinable factors go into the making of the total personality of an individual, and the total personality counts heavily in the technique of a professional broadcaster, which remains something of an art. Not that the total personality of a successful professional is always attractive. It can be, and sometimes is, downright abrasive, but it is never guilty of being dull.

Voice timbre might possibly be analyzed scientifically. A graphic representation of the sound wave pattern might reveal to the practiced eye the overtones which cause it to be pleasing or annoying. When we hear a voice, we all have an idea whether it is attractive, repulsive or in between. I haven't noticed too much disagreement among people about this. Although this is not strictly voice timbre—often the difference is really degree of eloquence—vocal quality, unlike modern art, is automatically discernible to most listeners, without any special training on their part.

Given a certain amount of voice quality, which need not be impressive, the prospective broadcaster, in analyzing his qualifications, must look at the other requisites. While the voice quality is almost completely God-given, the use of the voice in speech is to some extent teachable. Schooling in this is of real worth, as is exposure to speakers and personalities of merit.

Appearance is often overestimated. If it is your consuming desire to play the role of Adonis in a TV play, then, of course, a very specialized appearance is important, and frustration is inescapable if you are too old, too bald, too fat, too young. But almost any appearance (barring disfigurement of a kind cosmetic art cannot hide), backed up by other desirable qualities, will be more than adequate to a personality career. Television has added strength to the old saying: Handsome Is as Handsome Does.

The importance of authority as a quality cannot be overestimated. Here is a real indefinable. It is believed certain characteristics contribute to it—ease of manner, conviction, persuasiveness, familiarity with the material. Undoubtedly this is so. But I have seen people broadcast who were not ill at ease, who believed what they were saying, who spoke with earnestness, and who were beyond a doubt familiar with their subjects, and yet had little or no authority.

One of the most curious broadcasts I ever listened to was given by Albert Einstein just after the end of World War II. There can scarcely be any question of this man's sincerity, or his depth of understanding. But quite apart from an accent that rendered his English almost unintelligible, there was a lack of conviction about his delivery that scattered the attention focus and made his meaning difficult to capture. He lacked the technique, apparently, of articulating his thoughts and projecting his personality. Conversely, I remember one radio announcer on a network staff who seldom knew what his script said, who had to ask pronunciations and meanings of many rather common words, who did not necessarily believe what he read and didn't really care if his listeners believed it. Yet in spite of this, he had so much authority in his delivery that he was and is an excellent and high-paid radio announcer. I believe this particular phenomenon is restricted to radio. Television involves other modes of communication—the eyes, motions, body attitudes—and phoniness of certain types cannot survive visual presentation.

Most techniques useful in personality projection are quite rudimentary. To start with, facing the camera is a necessary step in establishing contact with the viewer. It sounds facetious, but animals and motion picture actors have trouble with this one. The latter have been trained to avoid eye contact with the camera. The former just don't care. Second, speaking into the microphone, even when it's out of sight over your head, is important to being heard. Other factors include grooming, a knowledge of what clothing looks best in TV, and knowledge of the right make-up for you. Here is a tricky one. You can appear without make-up, but somehow the medium almost always alters your real appearance, and you don't win. Or you can get make-up of the kind and in the amount that will make you appear on TV exactly as you appear in person without it. Or third, you can call on the skill of the make-up artist to make you look younger or older or prettier or more handsome or more wise. It's my opinion that the second of these choices is the most honest. This is an example of distorting fact to convey truth. I have no condemnation of the third choice. The person who caps his teeth or has his face lifted or wears a toupee is no fraud. No more than the man who shaves, and who would otherwise have a beard. Or the lady who diets, who would otherwise be fat. If it is part of your personality to strive to look good on the air, then it is quite honest to take advantage of cosmetic art and look the best you can.

What are the techniques of *personality* broadcasting? How can they be honest or dishonest? Must one never lie when broadcasting?

Slavish adherence to a simple commandment about telling the truth is not a proper technique for a mature person to consider. The clown who laughs when his heart is breaking is acting out a lie. If I were to go on the air with a headache and ignore it, even to a point of saying I felt fine, in strict fact I might be deceiving the viewing public. I don't think I have to say that there is no deception here of the kind that can undermine integrity. This white lie is voiced millions of times a day in every country on the globe. Evil intent is the only substance of a real lie. Inasmuch as a truthful answer is not usually welcome when an amenity concerning one's well-being is voiced, it is more reprehensible (since it may depress the inquirer) to say you feel terrible than to set forth the white lie of feeling fine. Intent, operating within a frame of custom and usage, makes the truth or the lie.

Intent is a highly personal, subjective thing. Each person may draw the line between Wrong and Right, between Harmless Deception and Outright Fraud at a different place. And the line is under constant pressure from Expediency, which justifies moving it by whispering like Iago in the subject's ear that the end justifies the means. And so the preservation of integrity is not so simple as anchoring one's line on some rock. It is a dynamic problem of holding the line against the temptation to wink at practices that may have become tradition, against the scorn of sophisticated colleagues, against increasing personal gain, against the feeling that the public doesn't really care (a false feeling, but one that creep up on you). Occasionally tragedy can make you glad you held the line.

The Congressional hearings on TV quiz practices in October of 1959, revealed painfully how people who deal constantly with the public and its entertainment interests can lose touch with important aspects of public temper. The producers of these shows had increased control to a degree that put them far out on a rotten limb. Was there evil intent here? I don't think so. These men are not villains. The programs' sponsors had allocated funds as prize money to begin with. Nothing was stolen from the companies. And no money was taken from the viewing public. But something was. If the public is to trust this medium in matters that are important, it must be able to trust it in matters that may not seem important to some producers. Again the matter of separating the real from the unreal. It is not enough to point out that public or private funds were not tapped in this deception. Had it been labeled drama, then there'd have been no deception. But obviously labeling the quizzes as dramatic fare would have defeated the whole purpose. The reasons for the high rating, the urgent pulling for a favorite, is that people watching believed they were rooting for a real person, and not an actor. Therefore the commodity that was tapped and drained was a human fluid made up of credulity, curiosity, empathy and compassion. Even the most enlightened society finds this fluid in less supply than demand, and resents any waste of it. To be duped is always annoying. To be duped by someone trading on your more tender qualities is infuriating. It is not second guessing to view the harvest reaped by such deception without surprise.

When the trend of daytime TV began a few years ago to veer away from variety programs and toward games, I had serious doubts about whether I belonged at all in the daytime schedule. I looked at many properties—all games. A few of them did not want me. Many of them would have made use of me, but not on my terms. More than once I suggested that if a show could not survive in competition without controlling the contests, the producers should abandon it and come up with one that *would* survive. I finally found one. "Concentration." If someone hadn't thought of it I might have turned my back on daytime television.

Even Concentration, although rigorously honest in its contests, shows more than traces of certain theatrical techniques applied almost automatically to broadcasts in the belief that they are "shows." The trade even calls them shows. These techniques are still tolerated by the public, but even the simplest viewer, while perhaps not openly critical of them, smiles inwardly and knows deep down that they are not necessary. The flavor of show business is much revered by people both inside and outside the trade, but I have long thought it unnecessary to force this flavor into everything that is broadcast.

Television is not "showbiz." Showbiz is one very important aspect of television, but there are many broadcasts that simply are not shows and shouldn't be made to seem so.

Specifically this applies to games and contests. And from what we've seen and from what I'd gathered long before from viewers' attitudes, it wasn't just that it's not necessary to dress up game broadcasts in showbiz clothes, it's bad for what the broadcast aims to do.

The proscenium arch, the spotlight, the fanfare—all point to something beguiling, something delightful, something offering escape from our cares—something *not real*. And there's the rub. Reality is precisely what the game broadcast wants most to convey, if it's honest, and if it is to be accepted for what it is. Not make-believe. And yet on many of the most real and earnest broadcasts—in fact on almost everything but straight news and sports, the industry will floodlight and stage and carry on like a troupe of the most improbable mimes.

Whom are they kidding with the gimmickry? Whom do they beguile with the panoply? Or with the narrow showmanship they find necessary to inject into an atmosphere of reality? The trade, that's whom. In the same way that fishing lures are designed to attract the angler at the counter of the sporting goods store, the industry follows a tradition that's become brittle in a few short years, dressing up every broadcast as a show whether it is or not. The client, and to a certain extent the public, has come to expect it.

This led to a confusion between what is a show and what is an event or game. The very words "quiz show" applied by the trade to a broadcast game (such as "Concentration") indicate the error. When real people struggle for real prizes in a real and honest setting, although it is in a sense an exhibition, it is like the gladiatorial contests, which the ancient Romans, you remember, were proper enough to call games.

Those vestiges of showmanship that Concentration displays are neither a threat to its acceptance as an honest broadcast, nor are they considered essential to interest on the part of the viewer. They are part of a tradition that does not need to be discarded immediately for the sake of avoiding an appearance.

Long ago Jack Farren (producer of the program) and I decided that there is no other criterion to be considered in making decisions concerning the show than whether the event or action is right and fair—that the avoidance of the appearance of evil, although desirable, is not to come into consideration at all if it clutters the prime motivation. We agree we would rather see the show destroyed holding to the right, than see it continue in any divergence from the right. It is gratifying to see the strength that has grown from such a policy. Concentration has weathered litigation, investigation, the possibility of terror on the part of its advertisers. It has also survived one bit of outright pressure.

A lady had come on the show and won, among other prizes, two automobiles. It was discovered immediately after her appearance that she had falsified her application regarding the amount of elapsed time since her last appearance on a prize program. As she was ineligible, the prizes which were not yet delivered, were withheld. Her attorney felt we might be susceptible to pressure in view of the effect publicity was having on many of the shows. He suggested that if we delivered the prizes anyway and forgot about her falsifications, they would not go to the papers with a story that we reneged on prizes. There was a feeling in one quarter that it might be best to accede and avoid the possibly devastating effect of publicity of this kind. But the final decision was to stick with the facts and act accordingly. Some papers printed her story, but there was no noticeable effect on the show.

NBC's decision not to panic and dump all game shows when some were shown to be rotten, but to cull out the bad ones and stand behind the good ones, was a long-range view not universally adopted by the trade—unfortunately. A question which may still be in the minds of many, is this: if NBC has the integrity not to tolerate a fraud program, and the foresight not to destroy a good one—why, then, did NBC have shows on the air that were not what they seemed to be? I will tell you why.

Many months before the investigations, the government had explicitly forbidden the networks to have a hand in the production of more than a certain number of their own shows, on grounds that it was a restraint of trade and a monopoly. It amounted to instructions not to interfere with outside packagers who brought shows ready-built to the networks, often with entire production crews. In many cases, if there were suspicion of chicanery, the people with the network were unable to pry into the state of affairs without breaking the law by "meddling" with the packagers' programs and therefore making the network a monopoly.

I don't believe the press, in the intoxication of its delight at such a field day as the investigations provided, did much to throw light on some of the facts. Particularly in those cases where the facts tended to mitigate the circumstances for broadcasters, and thus take some of the sting out of the blast against them.

10

Two Boys and a Still

One of the most important factors in developing a technique is discipline. Technique is really nothing more than disciplined freedom.

As has often been observed in acting, the technique is missing at first, then present and conscious, and at last present but unconscious. The novice feels no burden of technique because he has none, and his effectiveness (hence his talent) is at the mercy of chance. The hack feels keenly the technique he has learned and allows it, in his confusion, to eclipse what artistry he might otherwise have. The artist, finally, is unaware of technique because it is no longer something he uses, but something so much a part of him that his consciousness is left entirely free to address itself to his task. But unlike the novice, his talent is a directed force, never turned over to chance.

Without a scaffolding of discipline, there is nothing to climb on. A boat or an airplane moves forward by altering the momentum of the surrounding matter. The boat's screw, or a pair of oars, moves the water, and because each action has an equal and opposite reaction, the boat is moved. Life's disciplines constitute the surrounding matter, the momentum of which can be altered by the human spirit, allowing it to move forward. Discipline is the acceptance of laws. A set of rules is the matrix in which any patterned entity, from games to living things, has its very substance. The character of the game of chess is embedded in the rules of play. Permit an escape from the rules and you kill the game.

In the same way, a child in a permissive atmosphere is being destroyed at precisely that time of life when he should be acquiring this framework to climb on, these very implements of his real freedom. This is why I believe progressive education is a failure, despite sincere efforts of people who sought practical application of John Dewey's undeniably brilliant theories. In so doing, they were reacting against certain pompous aspects of Victorian authority concepts and, unfortunately, scrapped the good with the bad.

My maternal grandmother, although not pompous in her grasp and wield of authority, was certainly Victorian. Her mere presence produced, along with some awe, an atmosphere of certainty about Right and Wrong. Somehow her outlook, not only on moral issues, but on anything at all, had a character of stone and iron. As children we chafed, often, when immediate desires collided with buttress or beam of Grandma's rules, but we no more questioned their rightness than we would question their existence. Doubt may have been sprinkled occasionally on views of our parents, but not on Grandma's. An element of my adult wisdom, acquired through the second quarter of the twentieth century, tells me to regard Grandma's standards as quaint. I can hardly escape this attitude, since it is inevitable that each generation believes the preceding one to have been whimsical and the succeeding one to be stark daft. Perhaps what makes an objective view of that bygone age difficult for us in this generation is what Bernard DeVoto called "a neutral-colored thing that has been added unto us and is called, without value, sophistication." Grandma's outlook was handed to her by the age she lived in, and mine by the age I live in. Mine is better than hers only to the extent that it does not simply dismiss hers as quaint. If my outlook is too blind to evaluate the past and take the good from it, then I have not stepped forward, but only sideways.

She had her moments, even after my brothers and I were on the way to being mature. I remember once when Paul and I undertook to distill applejack in the summer kitchen. There was no sinister motive. I'm sure we knew that no one in our immediate family, and certainly none of the older folks, would be customers, or even applaud any success we might have. Never having tasted it, we had no thirst for it, and we had no intention of trafficking in illicit potables. It was simply a chemical challenge of the kind fifteen-year-olds cannot resist.

I'd like to take credit for the more enterprising moves since I have no moral feelings against our action, but truth will be served only if I say that it was Paul who studied the proper method of setting up the still and preparing the fermentation. He set about this with a zeal that, directed academically, would easily have had him delivering the valedictory at his graduation.

Being somewhat flamboyant in his approach to most projects, he favored compounding the drink with a number of aromatic agents. But for lack of those ingredients, and my efforts to keep everything as simple as possible, the whole thing might have been much more complicated —although just as futile.

We first bought a jug of sweet cider, and poured it into an old dish pan along with a quarter-pound or so of raisins we'd hooked from the pantry. As this mixture could be trusted to ferment by itself, we covered the dish pan with cheesecloth to keep out the curious, both human and animal, and started building the still. This proved to be more complex than we anticipated. We had four choices: (1) we could build a fire under the vat and burn down the summer kitchen for sure; (2) use a Bunsen burner or blowtorch, neither of which we had; (3) carry the whole thing, vat, head, condenser and receiver into the kitchen and arrange it on the stove—with no hope of not getting caught; or (4) set it up deep in the woods behind the big barn where revenuers would most certainly close in and bring us to justice.

"We might cut Dad in on it," Paul said.

"Are you kiddin'?" I asked. "He doesn't drink, and he knows we don't. He'd start asking why we're doing it in the first place."

This reasonable question could not have raised a semblance of reasonable answer, but even bringing it up to each other raised no real doubt in our minds. We knew, with the transcendent knowledge of faith, why we were doing it—because we had no reason on earth—and knowledge is always more solid when it isn't at pains to defend reason. Besides Dad had a practical turn of mind and his adult reasoning was, in our view, the frequent cause of failure.

Years before, with the object of building a glider, Paul and I had lashed an inch-thick board across the gunwales of a red wagon. Our plans included flights to Uncle Harry's on Jameson Street, and to Africa. The idea was for one of us to get in the wagon while the other pulled it at sufficient speed to make the board give wing lift. Then, off the ground it would go. We had made two unsuccessful test runs in front of our house one afternoon, when Dad arrived home. Breathlessly we told him what we were doing. After listening patiently, he gave us a dissertation on aerodynamics that wrecked the whole scheme. I offer as proof of this that after a dozen *more* test runs we had to give up, because not once did our winged wagon leave the ground. To this day both of us believe that if he hadn't happened on the scene, we might have established a flying corps of neighborhood plank-and-wagon gliders.

But back to the still. We decided to keep it in the summer kitchen and put a bonfire under the vat, protecting the floor with a large flagstone or a thick asbestos sheet, if we could find one. It was a bridge we never had to cross.

Every day we worked on the construction of the still, and checked the fermentation every hour. At first it was disappointingly slow, but after a few days it began a metamorphosis that was a wonder to watch. Paul had thought we ought to add sugar, but when the brew began to change, we abandoned that idea. We did add some apple peelings and cores by raiding the garbage, and by eating apples ourselves. We enjoyed the feeling that sitting there eating an apple could be work.

"We need enzymes," Paul said once. "They facilitate the hydrolysis of esters."

"What are esters?" I asked him, irritated because he could sometimes sound and act older than I could, although he was two years younger.

"Esters give the bouquet."

He could read up on the damnedest things and then

cast off fragments as though he'd known the subject so long he'd forgotten some of the details. I wasn't going to give him the satisfaction of asking what the bouquet was so I said, "Even in applejack?"

"Even in applejack."

He would speak airily of iris, hyssop, gentian, coriander and fennel as if he had phials of these in his back pocket, and as if any applejack worthy of the name should be properly dosed with these at the right moment.

"I never heard of applejack with that junk in it," I told him.

"That's just it," he rejoined. "We could *buy* ordinary applejack. Anybody can do that. Our applejack will be different from anybody else's! Bring a couple bottles of this stuff to the Halloween party —" he rolled his eyes. "Boy!"

"Yeah. You'd get kicked out of school."

The daily change that was taking place in our still was easily matched by the change going on under the cheesecloth. An ugly scum covered the surface of the cider now, dry in places, with multicolored furry radials and wartlike bumps. It would have gladdened the heart of a sorceress. Each day, rushing home from school, we found new bumps, and thicker scum, although the smell had leveled off in intensity. We worked feverishly on the apparatus, to have it ready before the mixture turned to vinegar.

We gave up trying to fit a Liebig condenser since we couldn't shape glass nor make any other material watertight. We went back to a metal plate, hoping to catch most of the distillate via a length of galvanized iron spouting that had served in other capacities, including that of a launching trough for Fourth of July rockets. We finally stepped back to admire our work. It was imposing. There were things attached to it which were nonfunctional, and to which Paul had given such names as "fractionating column" and "reflux pump," but it all added up to a handsome and basically workable distilling apparatus.

"All right, let's pour the stuff in and get 'er goin'!" I said, rubbing my hands.

"We forgot the stone," said Paul. "Or an asbestos sheet."

We had no plan, incidentally, for venting the smoke from this crematory. Even if we managed to avoid reducing the summer kitchen to embers, we'd certainly draw a fleet of fire engines to the scene before we had a thimbleful of applejack.

After making one last check of the fermentation, we agreed, without having any idea what we were talking about, that it had not yet turned, but would turn in another twenty-seven hours—just time enough for us to find the flagstone and get another day of school out of the way.

Late that afternoon we found a large piece of concrete from an old walk. We had to chip down some of the underside to get it flat, but at last it fit under the still, allowing about seven inches to build the fire.

Next day we rushed home from school to gaze with horror on an unparalleled tragedy—applejackdom had sustained a nasty blow. Our still was wrecked and our brew was gone. Gone! Dish pan and all. We looked at each other. Paul looked like a cowboy in the movies just before he spins around to show the fletched end of an Indian arrow sticking out of his back. He couldn't speak.

"Who do you s'pose would do that?" I finally asked in a quivering voice. I wanted to go to the house and try to find out, but that didn't fit in with our pattern of secrecy. Maybe we'd never know. That would be unbearable.

NBC Photo

Hugh as *Concentration* Chief on the popular NBC-TV game show.

At age 1 Hugh wins the Blue Ribbon in the Akron, Ohio, Baby Contest.

At 17 he graduates from the Shawnee High School, Lima.

With his brothers (*left to right*), Paul 6, Hugh 7, and Wallace 2.

Grandmother Hick, with Hugh's mother, Edith (*left*), and Aunt Kate (*right*).

Hugh's parents in 1956, at the time his father won the Westinghouse Award for the best essay on sound investment.

Westinghouse Photo

Hugh makes his first appearance as an announcer, WLOK, 1939.

Six years later before the NBC mike in Chicago, introducing *The Woman in White*.

Richard G. Kimble Photo

First broadcasts of the *Man-on-the-Street* show, WLOK, 1939, with Ed Braun (*right*) and an inquiring Boy Scout (*left*).

Interviewing Margaret Truman (*above*) and Cornelia Otis Skinner (*below*) on the *Home* program, NBC, 1956.

Manny Greenhaus Photo

NBC Photo

NBC Photo

Hugh combines hobby with profession. Here he is seen (*above*) with a piece from his antique gun collection and (*below*) with a "six-shooter" on the set of *Riverboat*.

NBC Photo

(*Above*) Hugh with Jack Paar, with whom he has spent more than 700 hours on the air and (*below*) as a guest of his friend Dave Garroway.

NBC Photo

NBC Photo

"Yours truly," Hugh Downs

We looked again at the corner of the summer kitchen where only yesterday we'd been set up and ready to go. The only thing still in place was the hunk of concrete we'd put down as a hearth. The vat of the still—a milk pail fitted with a large, improvised funnel to serve as an alembic—was on its side by the concrete, still reasonably intact, but bent. The head, the condenser, the receiver and those esthetic parts—the fractionating column and the reflux pump—were mangled beyond recognition. The spouting trough was wrapped around a supporting post near the center of the room, while the cheesecloth, partially dampened by the mixture, lay like a murdered rag doll where the dish pan had been.

"Must have been Dad," Paul said at last. His voice was flat, lifeless. He looked at me. "But where's the stuff?" he whispered.

"Who knows?" I said. "Maybe he drank it."

"S'pose he drank it and *then* —?" We looked at each other. Of course. It all made sense. Dad had found the still and the waiting brew, and although he had never touched a drop before, must have decided to sample it. Crazed by his first taste, he must have gone on a colossal bender, swilling down the remainder and then wrecking the joint. We'd better see if Mom was safe. We went in the house. Mom was in the kitchen.

"You're all right?" Paul asked her.

She looked at him sharply and then at me in the same way. I wanted to ask where Dad was, but couldn't get the words out.

"Boys, your grandmother wants to talk to you. She's in the parlor."

"Oh."

"Do you know what she wants to talk to you about?"

"I think so," I said. "Did she have Dad wreck the—the —still?"

She winced at the word and said, "Your father isn't home yet. Now I want you to know that if I had known about this, I'd have been just as upset. I might not have been as—as violent, but that doesn't mean for one minute that I condone such a terrible thing. Your father will feel the same way, I'm sure." She was speaking in a low voice, trembling slightly, and for a moment I thought she was on the verge of tears. She went on, "Now this is my house, and your father's. But you owe it, out of respect—boys, you *know* your grandmother is a member of the WCTU. This is an *awful* thing for her. And I'm not going to have her think I brought you up so badly that you'd do a thing like this. You're going to have to face her." Her mouth moved in a funny way that told me she was *not* about to cry. "Tell me one thing. You weren't planning to sell the stuff were you?"

"No!" we both said. "Honest!"

She put her hand to her mouth and said, "Now get in there and face your grandmother!" And I saw that she was struggling to keep from laughing. Neither of us could see anything funny about the situation since it was apparently a tragedy to Grandma and certainly a tragedy to Paul and me, who'd worked on this thing pretty hard. But we had a feeling that Mom was somehow on our side. We went in to face Grandma.

We sat down after mumbling hello Grandma and just waited. That was part of it. Waiting. She looked from one to the other of us and once we looked at each other and that was a mistake. We didn't have to be told it was a mistake. We just knew because her silence, unbroken, took on a more threatening character when we did that. They don't make matriarchs any more. Kids call their grandmothers by their first names now. I have the feeling that just *thinking* the first name of my grandmother in her presence would have drawn down instant retribution.

She didn't raise her voice. She never did anything to indicate that she had to behave in any special way to state her displeasure or assert her dominance. In calm, measured tones she spelled out the indictment. She described the horrors of the sodden life, documenting her thesis with a number of cases, all rather closely related to us. She detailed in particular how our mother's Uncle Henry was requited by Providence for getting plowed, which seems to have happened about twice a day, barring periods of a week or so when remorse and the DT's left him too weak to find a bottle and lift it. She quoted from the Bible, she thanked the Lord for His mercy in removing our grandfather from the scene and thus sparing him the sight she had had to look at this afternoon when she went to the summer kitchen. Then she told us what she had done.

Now Grandma was not a large woman. She was somewhat frail and about seventy-eight years old at the time. Yet a strong spirit can support frail flesh and fire it to incredible bursts of strength in the blast of indignation. She had smashed the machinery with a broom, mostly. But toward the end she had spied an ax, and this must have been an omen. While it didn't register with me at the time, now I'm glad for her that she was able to carry on in that inspired instant, as a sop to orthodoxy, in the manner of her ideal, Carrie Nation. She had next lifted the cheesecloth from the dish pan. To throw it out the window or door of that room would have withered the garden, she reasoned (and she was probably right); to spill it on the floor of the summer kitchen would, I suppose, have necessitated leveling the building. So she had carried it into the house and poured it down the sink. Paul gave a start when she said this, and she sharpened her tone as she went on, linking the devil to our actions. For a time I thought maybe the whole blame could be shifted to Satan, but that's because I was born in the twentieth century, which is weak on Responsibility. In Grandma's age you had the guts and the duty to walk alongside the devil and share his load of sin. Paul and I weren't going to be told by her that we weren't to blame. Since we had done this monstrous thing, we were the ones who had sinned. No one else.

She ended with the frank admission that it was not her job to mete out punishment since we were not her children, but it was her earnest hope that her daughter would pursue that end of things with the diligence she'd been raised to respect.

We finally left, subdued and grinning sheepishly at each other.

Mom made us show Dad, who wasn't too impressed because he hadn't seen the setup before. He may have figured we had made the still from pieces already bent that way. But he may have wondered as we did, how could Grandma, reared in such sheltered circumstances, never having had a look at any kind of distilling machinery, commercial or illegal, never having lived in the hills—how did she instantly spot and identify this apparatus of the devil?

Paul's theory is not to be considered. He found the idea of her having poured the brew down the drain so abhorrent that I think his mind snapped for a moment. He had hovered over that plasma for so long, with a concern that smacked almost of mother love, that I think he literally could not accept the idea of her having dumped it down the sink. Rather he preferred to believe that having sampled it, she was launched on a blind toot that resulted in heartbreak and destruction. He kept coming back to one piece of evidence which he thought clinched his argument.

"How else do you think a seventy-eight-year-old woman could wrap a piece of galvanized iron around a post like that?"

11

Take a Giant Step

My getting into broadcasting was almost accidental in a sense. Times were hard. I was living at home. Jobs were scarce and I had been hunting for several weeks. I had no real desire to work, but inasmuch as I free loaded—consuming spending money and as many groceries as an adult—my father had hinted that I might make some effort to pull my share of the load by getting into harness in the work-a-day world. His exact words were "Get a job." For a time he regarded my daily failure to find work with some suspicion, although he knew businesses were not sending personnel people out to snare passers-by on the sidewalk.

On a day in early June when Fate was to click a key tumbler in its lock of life for me, I had just returned from my twenty-sixth failure. A roofing company had been reported to need someone for something. On my way to the roofing company, I pondered what use it could find for a fellow who knew nothing about roofing and could boast an equal amount of insight and experience in any field you could mention. What earthly reason could they dredge up for hiring me, unless they were sitting around thinking up ways to get rid of money? After speaking briefly with a Mr. Ventura whose office was a lean-to badly in need of reroofing, I had the feeling that he was struck, on meeting me, with the folly of having advertised the job in such a way as to attract just anyone. I felt apologetic, as any roofing ignoramus should after taking up the valuable time of a roofing don.

Let me say that although the prospect of steady work loomed ahead of me with pronounced repulsiveness, the effect of gradually realizing that I had no place whatever in the productive life of the nation was a mood of great gloom.

On this day I arrived home determined to pack up and light out. I didn't know where, since the whole country was probably the same, and in any other country I'd be a foreigner. The trouble then, was with the world, yet I didn't care to leave it—at least not in the way of a suicide, who has to take pot luck on his destination. I felt trapped.

My mother asked me to go after milk. We bought it by the gallon in those days. There was a milk depot downtown where you could fill gallon jugs for less than four times the quart price. I took the empty jug to the car. The milk depot was a few feet from the studios of the radio station, which had originally used the call letters WBLY. For this reason and because for a time the staff had played phonograph records on a turntable of erratic speed, it came to be called "Wobbily." With its new owners, new facilities, and new call letters, nobody called it "Wobbily" any more. They called it "the new radio station," even though it transmitted from the same tower on the same frequency.

A thought struck me. Perhaps my destiny was with this kind of work. The thing that struck me hardest at the time was that I thought it wasn't work. I was right. Much ardor can go into the building of a broadcast career. You can sweat and persevere and expend considerable anxiety over certain projects, and I've done it, but it has never been work to me; and it is unlikely it ever will be.

At any rate, when I parked the car, I took my empty jug into the lobby of the radio station instead of into the milk depot. I set it down by the receptionist's desk and cleared my throat. She was young, redheaded and brisk.

"Yes," she said. It wasn't a question—it was a statement. It made me feel as though I had asked something. Since I hadn't, I couldn't think of what to say so I cleared my throat again and stood there looking at her. By now she had turned around to face me, leaving her typing in a brisk, redheaded way that conveyed the impression that this kind of interruption seldom happened, and never happened with someone carrying an empty gallon milk jug. She was pretty. Her smile was a mixture of some real warmth and a lot of patronizing patience. A good receptionist can fold an arriving executive right into his own briefcase with a smile like that.

"I'd like to become an announcer," I blurted out.

I'll never know what her response would have been, for at that moment there appeared in a doorway leading back to the offices a tall woman of uncertain age. This personage asked me to repeat what I'd just said. As I did so she looked at the brisk young redheaded receptionist.

"I said I'd like—to become an announcer," I repeated in a lower tone. I looked around the lobby the way you do when you've fallen down outdoors and want to find out who saw you.

"You'll have to see Mr. Dougherty," the tall one said, still looking at the redheaded one.

"Is he in?" I asked.

"He'll be off the air in eight minutes," she said. "He's doing the news."

I picked up my jug and backed toward the door. Both of them watched me all the way, the tall one with her mouth actually half open. This made her look taller.

When I returned to the lobby the jug was filled. I hadn't left it in the car, because the car had no lock. Once again, when I confronted the receptionist, she stopped typing and turned around.

"Is Mr. Dougherty off the air?" I asked. "He had eight minutes to go about eight minutes ago and—I thought—" I trailed off, feeling ridiculous.

"He'll be out in another minute or so. Why don't you sit down?"

Leaving my jug by the desk, I sat down on a long leather bench with my back against a mural containing semiabstract representations of Fannie Brice as Baby Snooks, Jack Benny, Fred Allen and Joe Penner, among other things. The leather of the bench felt dry and electric. Meanwhile the receptionist had turned her red head; reaching briskly to a row of switches, she flicked one. The voice of Mr. Dougherty came abruptly and harshly through a grill high in the opposite wall. Having heard him before on the air, I now realized with something of a chill that behind that voice was an actual human being who breathed air, ate food and had a place he called home, although he must be eight feet high and insusceptible to pain or worry. Since he was at that moment somewhere near, he would presently appear in person. I fancied that his voice would come straight from his throat in amplified, crackling, electric fashion—that the merest amenities would issue forth like bulletins rushed from the wires. How was I to communicate with such a titan of communication?

At eighteen, labels are all-important. Because we have no leverage whatever on inner essences of things at that age, we label everything, and then, resoundingly confusing the label with the thing, we are certain we know all that's to be known about everything. That's about the only comfort the eighteen-year-old gleans from his uncomfortable position in life—the certain and complete knowledge that his knowledge is certain and complete. He accomplishes this with his labels. Let us not be too hasty to strip them off his world. They will peel and shred soon enough. He hasn't a chance in a hundred of winding up feeling he knows what they've been pasted on, anyway. I'm not speaking of illusions. I'm speaking of labels: where a doctor is simply a doctor, and not someone who rode in a baby carriage, and played marbles, and went to high school and then college, and decided to enter medicine, and made it. Where a broadcaster is a Big Voice, not disembodied, but clothed with flesh and mingling with ordinary folks for appearance's sake—even adopting flashy habits shared on a smaller scale with others, like throwing the clubs in the rumble seat of a high-powered pleasure car and roaring off to the links for a fast nine between programs. He's a Big Voice, and a Sport, but he's not quite of our species.

We probably never really give up our labels, but in maturing, we at least admit what they are, realizing that they encrust something unfathomable. Sometimes we are shaken when fissures occur in the crust and white-hot tentacles of raw reality are thrust up from volcanic depths —what label will stay on Leonardo? The concept of finite space? Christine Jorgenson? The cloudy but necessarily arbitrary line between complex chemical activity and simple life? The decision whether a two-headed human is two people sharing a body or a single soul with a spare head? It's much more comfortable just not to think about such things.

As Ben Dougherty finished the news, another voice came on identifying the station and urging people to join what he called a throng that appeared to be assembling at Kyle's Paint Store. The technique of both copy and delivery I would later be able to identify as threadbare, but now, as I remember the announcement, there was embedded in that sensual and unctuous tone an implied promise of positively shameless reward for those who dropped everything and rushed to Kyle's to select wallpaper in the riotous orgy of new patterns just uncrated.

The program which followed was produced by the Treasury Department. It wafted into the lobby with its opening strains until the brisk young redheaded one snapped it off. At that point, Mr. Dougherty appeared in the doorway with a sheaf of news copy.

He was of medium height, slightly stooped, and graying just over the ears. Nothing about his bland face suggested the authority that rang from his voice on the air.

"There's someone to see you," said the girl, doing something impressive, like sorting papers and simultaneously nodding in my direction.

I stood up.

I tried to smile in a manner at once debonair and ingratiating, an absolutely unemulsifiable combination. I don't know how it looked, but it felt like I might be doing a Stanislavski impression of a three-day-old lettuce sandwich smelling something unpleasant. That's the awful thing about shattered poise. You can be fully aware it's all down the drain, and yet somehow you bull it through as though you had planned it that way. Which inevitably makes it worse.

"I—ah—how do you do," I forced out, advancing on Mr. Dougherty with outstretched right hand. He had his news copy in one hand and two or three transcription discs in his other. Just as he was starting to shift the news script over in order to get his right hand free, I picked up my gallon milk jug, and, seeing he had a free hand, unaccountably handed it to him.

"I'd like to be an announcer," I said.

"I thought you were selling milk." He looked at the jug. "Is this a gift? Or a bribe?"

Even in my confusion I noted that the Dougherty voice, though recognizable, was human in dimension, lacking the electronic punch and crackle familiar now to the community.

"No." I said. "Or yes, you're welcome to it. If you want it. I just thought you'd probably say 'no'—to my idea about being an announcer, that is—and—I picked it up to leave."

He smiled, looked at the girl, and indicated the door to the offices by tossing his head. "Come on in," he said. "Hazel can guard your milk." He set the jug down at the edge of her desk. "She does it for everyone who comes in."

"It's in my contract," she said briskly.

"Now," Ben Dougherty said after we were seated in his office, "you're interested in radio as a career. You're not here because you think you can get rich in three months?"

"No."

"Good."

"Marge!" he called through the door. The tall one appeared, her mouth still partially open. Apparently every event she witnessed caused her considerable astonishment. Or perhaps the world shocked her perpetually. There are people like that. "See if you can round up some different types of copy. This young man—your name—"

"Hugh Downs," I said.

"Mr. Downs wants to audition for announcer." She disappeared and he turned again to me. "Normally we audition on Fridays, but I might as well hear you now."

I thanked him. Presently Marge returned with four sheets of paper, which she handed him and which he turned over to me after looking at them briefly.

"Now," he said, rising, "read through these to yourself in the studio, and then read them aloud, one after the other when you get a signal. Follow me."

We went back through the reception room, past Hazel, past my milk jug, past the murals of Jack Benny and Fred Allen and Fanny Brice and Joe Penner, and through a door that led to the smaller of two studios. These flanked a common control room, with glass panels yielding a view of each from the console control panel. Inside, Dougherty showed me where to sit and how far to stay from the microphone.

As he left he said, "For God's sake, don't try to announce. Just read it for the meaning, the best you can. Start when the red light comes on."

Suddenly I was alone. In the hush I could hear only my own breathing and the faint grinding of a large electric clock on the far wall. Over the door was a single red bulb. A foot and a half in front of me was an RCA 77-B on a desk stand. Its ribbon was assigned for the next few seconds to send fluctuations of electric current through a cord and into a plug in the wall, and thence to equipment in the control room, which in turn would send it out to activate a speaker in Dougherty's office in such a way as to create the impression that my voice was making the sound. Would this electronic metamorphosis put into my voice the quality of authority that stamps the real broadcaster? Would it filter out amateur sounds? Should I really take his advice to speak naturally, or should I try to sound the way I think I ought to in order to pass the audition? Might they throw the wrong switch and put my voice on the air? What if I accidentally swore? How can men face dangers like this daily? What kind of nerve do I have to sit here and associate myself with Colossi like these? How do I dare, a timid poltroon still rooted in the home town, to aspire to the ranks of warriors from Toledo and Cincinnati—whose souls and outlook must have been forged in homes destined to produce leadership and courage incarnate?

I heard a voice come faintly through the glass to the control room. It was the announcer at the controls, reading a commercial. I looked at the copy I had on the table. The red light would come on soon, and as yet I hadn't looked this over! Quickly I scanned the announcements. The first one was a one-minute spot detailing the merits of a shoddy roadhouse at the edge of town. Naturally, the announcement didn't include the word "shoddy" among its descriptive adjectives. Perhaps it wasn't shoddy from the inside at night—I had never been there—but from the outside in the daytime it didn't look like anything to broadcast about. The second paper was the announcement I had heard just after Mr. Dougherty's newscast—the one about Kyle's Paint Store. The third was a page of news from a teletype machine. I started to read through them, glancing at the red light after each line. Midway through

Kyle's announcement I heard a tapping on the control room glass and the fellow inside looked the question "Are you ready?" at me. I nodded yes, which was a lie, and he pointed to the red light. In a few moments it came on, and I started.

When I had finished I sat there. The clock ground on. It was heedless—as I was ignorant—that it was grinding out the closing seconds of an era that started when Time itself began, and during all of which I had never been a professional broadcaster. The earth had cooled and its steaming seas spawned scum and crustaceans, reptiles, mammals and man, and never had there been a broadcaster named Hugh Downs. And it had got along fairly well up to now, except for the Inquisition and the Roaring Twenties, and a few things like that.

Ben Dougherty opened the studio door. He came in and closed it, and sat down across the table from me. He picked up my papers, looked at them, and shook his head.

"You may have been a little nervous—" he began.

"I was."

"But in spite of that, it really was quite bad."

I swallowed. Two thoughts marched into my mind and sat down opposite each other. Number one—it was stupid to have come here with no knowledge of the profession, and since I was bad even allowing for nervousness, I must have been lacking in aptitude, too. Number two—I could talk. My voice was not unpleasant and my desire to do a good job should have shown through any lack of technique. Perhaps Ben Dougherty was not sensitive enough to spot potential. Therefore the hell with him and his station. There were other stations in the country. These two thoughts glared each other to a standstill.

"But then," he continued, "the reason it was bad is not

a hopeless one. It's because you didn't take advice. If you struck me as the kind that could never take advice I wouldn't be talking to you now. I'd be closing the outside door on you and wishing I hadn't wasted five minutes."

He slid Kyle's commercial around the mike to my side. "I'll give the advice again. Tell me any one fact out of this copy that you pick out. Don't read it—paraphrase it."

I stared at it.

"Just one point you think they want to get across to the public."

"Well," I said, "they seem to want everyone to go there and buy wallpaper." I read on down. "And they want to stress that if you don't get there soon you'll miss out on something good."

"Excellent!" he snapped. "Go for meanings. The only reason for saying words—for saying them at all—is for a *meaning*. If you go on the air to get the sound of your golden voice to the millions, or to fill a minute, or to showcase some literary structure, you'll never be an announcer. This guy has paid his dollars for you to convince listeners he has something worth-while in his store. He doesn't give a damn for the sound of your voice—and the truth is the only time your voice really sounds good is when you are concentrating so hard on the meaning of your message that you've forgotten you're using your voice. You hear what I'm saying?"

"Yes."

"Well, the length of time it'll take you to become an announcer will be the length of time it takes for that to soak in. Read the last paragraph again."

I cleared my throat as I looked at the copy. " 'So hurry down to Kyle's while the selection lasts. Kyle's is at Main and Collett streets.' "

"Now do it without reading. Look at me and tell me to hurry to Kyle's and worry a little that I might be too late."

Good Lord, I thought, I can't look a grown man in the eye and be earnest about something he knows damned well I couldn't care less about. Another thought came into my mind to play devil's advocate to that one—you can walk out of here, pick up your milk jug and thank Hazel for guarding it, and take the milk home to your mother in this pleasant town in this free country. Forget the inferno of show business. Seek the security of job hunting among the roofing companies of the community, never be a target of public attention, and no one will ever say you've done anything wrong because you won't have. On the other hand, if you stick with this ridiculousness, you'll be doing so out of sheer obstinacy or hamminess, or both. You're at a fork in the road; one lane is lit a little brighter than the other. Make up your mind.

I looked at Ben Dougherty across the microphone and said softly, "You better get over to Kyle's right away, Mr. Dougherty." Something in the look on his face made me add, probably to keep from laughing, "and buy some wallpaper. Please. They need the business!"

He stared at me. I couldn't tell whether he was *trying* to figure out the extent of my flippancy and my failure to take the whole business seriously, or whether he had already figured it out. If he had, he was way ahead of me, for I couldn't have explained my behavior to save my life.

Suddenly he chuckled. He gathered up the papers and stood up. "Get out," he said. "And don't come back till Monday. Can you start then, on a part time, daily basis?"

"I—I sure can!"

"Three hours a day to start with. It pays seven dollars and fifty cents a week. Maybe it won't be long till you can get a full shift. In any case you're a member of the staff. A deal?"

We shook hands.

The clock ground right on as though 5:25 PM EST May 18, 1939, were just another point in the infinite moments of history. Time chewed up that second unconcernedly as it had chewed up the instant Caesar was stabbed, and as it was to chew up the moment the first A-bomb flashed to furious vapor over the southwestern desert.

When I picked up my milk jug, Ben Dougherty explained to Hazel that I was a new member of the staff. She said something perfunctorily congratulatory but flavored with the implication that he'd made a monster boner. But that was because she was brisk and redheaded, as well as young and pretty. I forgave her.

My father's reaction was typical. "Spend the rest of the week looking for a job," he said. "If you can't find one, go with the radio station."

That was twenty-one years ago.

I never found a job.

12

Ben Dougherty

Ben Dougherty never held a grudge any longer than it took him to get rid of one. That could be anywhere from ten seconds to ten years, depending on the accessibility of the person he was mad at. He couldn't stay mad at anyone who was around him all the time.

Ben conducted a man-on-the-street broadcast every noon. It was one of two broadcasts he did every day. The other one was the late afternoon news. Working conditions on the man-on-the-street program were very uncomfortable, and the show bored Ben, but he did it because the sponsor liked him.

There are two ways of broadcasting a "remote." One involves paying the telephone company for lines to which you attach your microphones; they pipe it back to your studios. The other way is to string your own lines. Normally it is cheaper to pay for telephone lines than to put up your own, even if you're merely going to do a remote broadcast from across the street. By the time you paid for wires, strung them in compliance with local ordinances (not crossing a thoroughfare, not stringing wires that might contrive to hang people on bicycles or in convertibles), you would have paid much more than simply arranging with the phone company for a leased line.

But in the case of our man-on-the-street program, it was actually cheaper to do the remote without calling in the phone company. The reason was that we were on the eleventh floor of a bank building, while the broadcast was on the ground floor just outside the drugstore, eleven stories straight down. Since we had a studio extension cord just about long enough to reach, we said to heck with the phone company, we can save some money. This cord, remember, was *just about* long enough. When the male end of the cord was plugged into the studio outlet nearest the window, the female plug swung disconsolately a good ten feet above the sidewalk. This was not a big obstacle, however. The cord on the microphone itself, which Ben always took down on the elevator with him, was nearly fifteen feet long, so that made up the difference. But connecting it required a ritual that no life insurance company would have countenanced. I had to let the extension down the side of the building to its full length, and then, holding the plug at my end, lean out the window as far as I could without following it down. When I had done this, Ben could reach up and just make the connection—that is, plug the mike into the extension. Once this was accomplished I would pull the cord back up just far enough to plug it into the studio wall. Now the splice, where Ben had plugged his mike into the extension, was far above his head out of reach, but it didn't matter since he had plenty of the mike's own cable to move around with.

It was my duty, on that shift, to do the station break following his man-on-the-streeter, hook up to the network or go to a solid quarter-hour transcription. After that I was supposed to unplug the extension from the studio outlet and let the cord down (again as far as I could reach out the window) until he had unplugged the mike. Then I would pull the extension back into the studio and stack it in a neat coil. All well and good. Except that I forgot him the second day I had this assignment. He finished the program while I blandly stayed in the control room reading the paper, or something. He went inside to the drugstore, parking the mike behind some papers on a newsstand just inside the door. From there he called me on the phone. He kidded me about forgetting him. I thought he was very nice about it, considering the day had been so hot the air rippled over the pavement. Ben had mentioned once that the pavement was so hot during those fifteen minutes that if he didn't sort of prance around, the soles of his shoes began to set fire to his socks. First he would get someone to interview, then he would maneuver the victim into a position where he could stand in the other fellow's shadow.

This day had been brutal. When I got the phone call reminding me of what I'd forgotten, I felt terrible. But as I say, he was nice about it. I quickly lowered the extension, saw him reach up and disconnect his mike, then I pulled up the cord. Afterward I apologized to him. He said forget it, and I did. I mean I forgot again the very next day. Once more, I was reading the newspaper, and after about ten minutes of the next program, Ben appeared in the doorway and asked what the hell was going on.

"What do you mean?" I asked innocently.

"I mean I had to leave the mike in the drugstore to get up here. Why the hell can't you remember to let that line down as soon as the program's over?"

I made some lame excuse about station break and the

chores that crowd on one in the hectic period between programs. He didn't even stay to hear the end of it. He stomped out after complaining that today was hotter even than yesterday and he couldn't get in the shade till I had let the line down. I felt really silly this time.

Will you believe it that the next day, still hotter than the two preceding ones, I stayed in the control room and forgot him *again*? I wasn't reading a newspaper this time. I was talking on the transmitter phone to Burt Shefflin, the chief engineer, who together with his assistant, made up our engineering staff. I was talking to Burt about hunting. He was from Pennsylvania and his burning ambition was to shoot a ring-necked pheasant. They were very scarce in his part of the country, but he had seen several specimens since he got here last month and boy would he love to plug one of those babies. Someday he wanted to bring his shotgun in to the studio. Although it was still nearly four months until hunting season, we were talking about it as though the opening day were a matter of hours away.

Suddenly Ben Dougherty, damp and purple, stood there in the door, saying nothing.

I looked at him and, after about three seconds for a slow take, said, "Oh, good Lord!"

"Yes, good Lord," he said, clenching his teeth, the sides of his jaws going white. "I—just don't know what to say."

I was really embarrassed. His shirt was sopping wet from perspiration. He kept standing there as though somebody might come in from one of the offices and hand him something to say. I didn't know just what to say either. I kept shaking my head and finally muttered, "Boy, I don't know what's wrong with me." This may have given him what he wanted in the way of a lead, for he exploded.

"I know what's wrong with you! You've got a big puff

ball for a brain, that's what's wrong with you! It's hot out there! Hotter than it's been yet this year, and I have to stand out in that furnace for a quarter-hour *anyway*, yakking with those oafs about how hot it is, and that makes it hotter! Then I wait, thinking, *this* time he'll remember and let the cord down and I can get inside before I have a goddam stroke! But does the stupid son of a bitch remember? No! And an eighty-five-dollar RCA salt shaker is sitting down there right this minute in a nest of newspapers, and if some free booter comes along and steals it *you're* gonna pay for it—get that?"

That seemed fair. I calculated swiftly and realized that I'd work for three months for nothing at my present salary to cover the cost of that microphone. But I had a sense of relief that he seemed to be getting it out of his system without actually killing me.

He went back to his office. I didn't know him well, and was afraid he might have put me on some kind of permanent list. But when I saw him again an hour later he was as pleasant as if nothing had happened.

Now if the story could only be ended here, it would be more compatible with normal reader credulity. But it is more important that it be compatible with truth. And so I must report the final, incredible chapter. I only ask you to bear in mind that truth *is* stranger than fiction.

Next day when I came in, Ben had gone down on the other elevator, so I didn't see him. I relieved Lew Rommil, who had signed on, and whose last chore was to get the man-on-the-street show started. He had leaned out the window and stayed alive to pull the extension back in far enough to plug it into the wall socket. And now he was through. Today wasn't like the last few days. It was Friday and it was raining.

I sat there for awhile after Lew left, looking out the window at the misty outlines of the other side of Lima's public square, blurred in the rain, and listening to Ben's struggle to find people he could talk to. His monologue went something like this: "—well, we'll have somebody along shortly. It sure is a foul day! A real nor'easter! It's a relief, after that heat we've been having, but it's coming down now with a vengeance! There's a fellow down the street coming up this way. See if we can get him. We get a little shelter here in the doorway, but not much. It seems to blow every direction at once. Ha, ha! Hey, fella! Over here! (Pause.) C'mon over here! We'd like to talk to you a moment. Here he comes. Right here! Hey! C'mon back! A little rain never hurt anybody! (Pause.) Well, we'll get somebody else after bit. Now let me tell you a little about our sponsor's product."

The whole quarter-hour was like that. When it ended I read the short break copy and introduced the next show, which was the fifteen-minute Treasury Department program. While I was leading into that, Hazel appeared and waited till I'd finished, then reminded me that I hadn't finished my log from yesterday. Ben had said the R.I. (radio inspector) could drop in at any moment and the log was expected to be up to date. I got busy on the log. After that I typed some schedules and wrote a report on a remote from the Locomotive Works. Following the Treasury program, I read another short announcement at break time and joined the net. Ben Bernie was on from New York—the Astor, I think.

It must have been 12:40 or so when I decided I was thirsty. Incoming network programs were gain-controlled by the engineers at the point of origination, so I could leave then if I didn't go too far away—sort of like auto pilot. As I started out into the studio to get to the lobby, something didn't look right. I stared for a moment before I realized that what didn't look right was the extension cord. It was not coiled up in the corner; instead, one end was plugged into the wall and what was visible of it "snuck" up over the window sill and out into the rain down the side of the building.

A cold chill came over me. My blood turned to ice and my knees sagged. "Oh, no!" I whispered. Rather than admit, even to myself, that I could have forgotten this operation for the fourth consecutive day, I cast about for some other explanation. Someone else must have put it back up after I had taken it down. They were experimenting or something. It wouldn't work—I knew very well I had never taken it down.

I looked through the glass into the lobby expecting to see Ben advancing with a machete or a machine gun. Nothing. Hazel wasn't even at her desk. Determined not to panic, I moved cautiously toward the outer door. The door from the lobby to the offices was open and I peeked in. No sign of anyone. At length I got up nerve enough to look in Ben's office. Vacant. I heard Hazel then, talking to Marge, the tall bookkeeper. I went to Marge's office.

"Know where Ben is?" I croaked.

"No," said Hazel.

"You look sick," said Marge.

"I am. I mean, do you know where he is?"

Marge jumped up. "Is something wrong on the air?" She always gave the impression that she didn't think I could cut it, and that at any moment she would have to rush in and straighten out some emergency, big or little, probably caused by the error Ben Dougherty had made in hiring me. I used to think Hazel felt the same way, but I no longer believed that. She always seemed amused, although she didn't seem so superior any more. Still brisk, still redheaded, still pretty, but a little friendlier. I wanted to confide in her what the problem was, so she might take it down in shorthand. Then the world would at least know my side of it before I was lynched. I went back and looked again. The cord was still there. I had hoped that maybe I had hallucinated a little, and that when I returned to the studio I'd find the extension all coiled up neatly in its corner. I went through the control room and sat down. It was now 12:45, a full half hour after the end of the man-on-the-street program. No Ben. He had undoubtedly parked the mike in the newspaper rack again. Possibly—yes, this must be it! He had become so upset and angry that, afraid he might do something really rash, he left the mike in the drugstore and just went home! A good, sound, rational decision to make on a rainy day when you're violently upset. Andbody'd do that. Anybody.

Anybody but Ben Dougherty. Where the hell was he?

I went back to the studio. There was the extension, threading from the wall plug up to the window sill, out through the slightly opened steel frame and down the side.

On a whim I opened the window wider, poked my head out into the rain, and looked down. There, standing close by the building, was Ben. I couldn't believe it at first. I drew back inside like a murderer who has seen the corpse again, perhaps in a new place. I unplugged the extension, and leaned out the window with it.

I saw Ben's hands go up to grab the knot and unplug the mike. Then he disappeared into the building. I pulled the extension in, coiling it as I did so. I coiled mechanically, with no thought of the wetness of the cord, or of my clothes getting damp and dirty from it. I went back into the control room and pulled the typewriter over. Putting a piece of paper in the roller I typed out, "I resign. I'll leave today. . . ." Then I stopped and took the paper out. I heard the elevator door.

The next sounds I heard were sloshy sounds.

He had decided to outwait me, if it took me all day to discover that I'd left him there. He didn't even go into the drugstore, which he could have done. He stood there in the pouring rain and wouldn't budge! There is something kind of admirable in that mixture of stubbornness and stupidity.

I thought of closing the control room door, but that was silly. I faced him as he came in.

The puddle at his feet grew as he stood still in the doorway. His hat looked like a small fox that fell into a sluice gate at Bagnell Dam—the brim was down all around and stuck to his cheek on one side. His chin dripped water onto his shirt, which dripped it onto the floor. His trousers clung to him. He looked like something the police might have fished out of a reservoir.

In spite of some very real terror, I realized I was about a half a breath away from laughing. The only thing I could think of to say I said, partly to keep from laughing.

"Thank heaven you're safe!" I said. "We've been so worried about—"

"Get out!"

"Am I fired?"

"No, you're not fired. You're going to live to take over this rotten show, and I'm going to schedule it only when it's a hundred and ten or pouring down rain or snow! You'll be scheduled on it this winter if it gets to twenty below! You're the baby that'll stand down there until brass monkeys talk back to you in a high voice! And do you think I'll let the cord down for you?" His voice cracked on the last word and he stopped, realizing he was getting really hysterical. "No," he went on, in a softer tone, "I'll sit here in comfort and if you park the microphone anywhere and don't stay with it to guard it, no matter *what* the weather's like, *then* you're fired!" Shaking his head and flapping his arms like a tuckered awk, he turned away and headed for the door. "I'm going home and change. I may not be back." I wanted to tell him I was sorry, but it would have sounded watery, and that's the last thing he needed. At the door he turned and looked at me.

"How long might you have left me there?" he asked.

"I'll tell you if you'll tell me how long you'd have stayed."

"Forever," he snapped, "For the rest of my life. Which wouldn't have been too long. I was drowning." He smiled.

I smiled back. "I owe you something more than an apology," I said.

"Yes, you owe me a drink and a new suit. You can't afford the suit, and since you don't drink, it wouldn't mean much for you to buy one for me. So forget it."

He disappeared, and an hour later he was friendly again.

13
Hi Jinx
and Happenstance

A COMPILATION of broadcast fluffs, laid end to end, would reach from NBC New York, transmitting from atop the Empire State Building, to your receiving antenna, wherever you live.

Many of these are apocryphal. Some are embellished. Some are pure fact. I have seen and heard some of them at home, seen and heard others while monitoring incoming broadcasts on duty, and have been present at a few.

Slips of the tongue can be very funny, as well as very painful to the slipper at the time (and therein lies a much observed fact about certain types of humor).

One of the worst hazards of broadcasting is just to keep from laughing on certain occasions. Everyone has seen the comedian suddenly struck funny and unable to contain himself, but it is not always fate that reduces a performer to a quaking jellyfish of mirth. Perverse fellow workers succeed in doing it often; they attempt it even more often.

The most popular methods in radio include such things as setting fire to a newscaster's copy while he reads it—

then standing back to watch him go down in flames; undressing him, garment at a time, as he reads the news or a long piece of narration (he will usually assist the perpetrators of the prank in order to insure the smooth flow of words); staring or making faces at him; or holding up hand-lettered signs supposed to be funny. These methods are so old hat by now that broadcasters are more likely to be annoyed by them than uncontrollably amused.

There are some original ploys that are more effective—at least they worked with me. An engineer who had tried unsuccessfully to break me up during quarter-hour newscasts finally made it by putting his chin on the top of his control console, slipping off his shoes and putting one on each side of his face, soles out, as if he had his feet against his ears. Since he weighed almost three hundred pounds and this contortion would have been completely impossible, it got me. I recovered during the next story but was shaky for the rest of the broadcast. Another announcer on staff at NBC, with nothing better to do, put a reflector on top of his head, holding it so it did not actually rest on his hair. It looked something like a coolie hat, for the center had a hole in it for the bulb, which was not in it at the time. It looked funny and I smiled when I glanced up and saw it. He stood there as though he didn't realize it had failed to do me in. I went on with the news. After a bit I glanced up again and this time saw white smoke drifting up through the hole in the top of the reflector! He had stashed another fellow, a night clerk of minikin stature, behind him to blow cigarette smoke up the back of the metal hat. I went.

But the funniest things having to do with broadcasts are never planned. While I was program director of my home town station, I listened helplessly in my office as a staff announcer delivered a eulogy for a prominent department store owner who had died that afternoon, and proceded to dedicate a religious song to his memory. The song was "When Jesus Calls a Sinner Home." I don't think he ever understood quite what he'd done, but it so happened the department store owner was an Orthodox Jew. As a postscript I want to add that the store continued its advertising campaign with us, exhibiting the tolerance of an eighty-five-year-old establishment toward a year-old business in the same community.

The human mind, because it is capable of error, is a fit tool for the human soul. Our personality is shaped, I believe, by the aggregate of malfunctions in the mind.

At WDT in Detroit the announce booth had a very simple control for the announcer. A single button, pushed once, turned on the microphone. Pushed again, it turned *off* the microphone. Nothing could be more foolproof. The copy for a whole shift was put in order in a large looseleaf binder by the continuity department, then placed on the table in the booth. If there were changes, they were attended to by someone who came up from Continuity.

On a memorable day one of the announcers, an extremely meticulous chap named Ryerson who made only two errors in all the time I knew him (and these made up for all the times he should have goofed and didn't), had gone into the booth early. He always went earlier than the rest of us, who had developed the precarious habit of moving into the booth for station-break chores with hardly ten seconds to spare. It was Ryerson's custom, however, to go into the booth a full four or five minutes in advance of his assignment, checking things to see that they were right. He would then stand in the door, talking, until perhaps five or ten seconds to go. He had a sort of ritual, in fact. He would go into the booth, open the loose-leaf book to the correct announcement, place it on the table in precisely the correct spot, examine his tie in the double glass partition between the booth and master control, adjust his boutonniere, and finally turn to stand in the doorway, resuming any conversation that might have been left dangling. As soon as he heard the system cue, he would wheel around, close the door swiftly, jab at the button that turned on the mike and give the station call letters and the station-break announcement.

But on this day, which I am sure he will never forget if he lives to be a hundred and thirty, he had not taken account of a petite nymph from Continuity whose name was Geraldine, a courier frequently seen on our level, for it was her duty to take care of changes in our book. Today she had slipped in behind Ryerson as he stood in the doorway chatting, and after whatever alterations she had effected in the loose-leaf, had closed it. She slipped out as shadowlike as she had come in, unaware that she had undone some important pre-broadcast preparations.

With that ever-alert inner ear that can ruin a nap for an announcer whenever chimes ring, Ryerson caught the system cue during one of his own sentences. He turned suavely from the lounge, closing the door in a graceful, self-assured manner. He even made a last-minute check of his tie.

What happened then I can only tell you step by step and say simply that this is *exactly* what happened. I can offer no explanation. Seating himself at the table, Ryerson turned on the mike by pushing the button, then said into it, "WDT, the Detroit News Station, Detroit." On the second Detroit he became aware that the book was closed and that his place was lost. Swiftly he jabbed the button, turning the mike off. Then he began windmilling through the book trying to find his place before time ran out and a paid spot went down the drain. In the middle of his frenzied paddling of pages, he reached up, turned the mike *back on,* said, "Jesus Christ!" and turned it back off, to go on flailing through the copy. Engineers came piling out of the woodwork. The lounge filled quickly with clerks, executive assistants, executives, and company officers, in that order.

Ryerson's report was a masterpiece of cloudiness. It included the opinion that the control in the booth was not functioning right, and a reference to having heard "—crosstalk on my monitor speaker that entailed profanity." He stoutly maintained he had been silent during the whole thing, trying to get the mike turned on, and that during those seconds he had heard some voice come in from somewhere with what could have been part of a sermon. The two engineers who had seen his lips move as the words came through, and who saw his face go whiter than his shirt, never said anything. His job was saved.

In Chicago a local newscast was sponsored for a long time by a big oil company. The newscaster was subject to occasional attacks of laryngitis, which could close in on him in a matter of minutes and leave him virtually voiceless. The announcer, long a favorite of the sponsor, had battled off and on with a drinking problem. He would sometimes show up for his broadcast quite bombed. His colleagues at the station frequently covered for him and kept him off the air if he were obviously too plowed to escape detection. As he was usually convinced that he could do the job well, this was not always easy. He argued in thick accents and with some belligerence against being replaced. Furthermore, if he walked a few blocks before coming to the studio, he gave the appearance, for the first few minutes, of being perfectly all right. But after standing still awhile, the fumes would rise and his sober pose would deteriorate. By the end of the program, if he hadn't been hustled out by friends, he might be unable to stand up at all.

The following historic broadcast was not relieved by any gesture of heroism. Most of the staff was either tied up in extra recording session or at dinner, and I listened to it in its entirety on my car radio eighteen miles from the studios.

Ray had come in, spoken to Stan Roeber in the newsroom, picked up his commercial copy and gone into the studio. The one remaining staff man had poked his head in the door of the newsroom and asked Stan, "Did Ray come in?"

"Yes," Stan said.

"Is he okay?"

"Yes, he looked fine. Spoke to me. He was walking straight."

"Everything under control, then," said the staffer. "I'm going to eat."

At two minutes to go, Stan gathered up his news copy and went into the studio. After settling himself before the table mike, he read a line for level check to the engineer in the control room.

"Did Ray come in here?" he asked.

The engineer said he'd come in and gone to the men's room. At forty-five seconds to go Ray returned, spoke pleasantly to Stan, cleared his throat and said, "Stand-by."

Stan had been having a little trouble with his voice earlier in the afternoon—just a slight huskiness, nothing more. He didn't know he was destined to get only six minutes into his news before it gave out completely.

The opening announcement went to perfection and Ray ended it with, "And now here with the headlines is Stan Roeber."

Stan did a minute and a half of highlights which went well in spite of a slight hoarseness that took the edge off the nuances he usually managed, but this was not noticeable on most radios. At the end of these briefs he returned it to Ray for the traditional word from our sponsor. Here was the first of two full-minute commercials Ray had to do. Within fifteen seconds Stan knew that something was wrong. Ray thrashed on manfully, but certain consonants were fuzzy or protracted and whole syllables slurred over.

"—at the service station wur the shine is dish—dishplayed that tells you," he was saying, weaving slightly from side to side, "—the gas-leen your car will thank you for. Now—" (Pause.) "back to Shtan Roebews—Shtan Roebers and the new—" as he finished, he grabbed the mike stand and for a moment threatened to drag it with him to the floor. Stan resumed in panic, signaling to the engineer, by pantomiming a phone call, that he was to summon help.

After another two minutes Stan's hoarseness had got to a point that made it hard to understand him. This seemed to rouse Ray, who moved to the table, sat down opposite Stan and took the copy away while he was reading it. He shook his head violently as though to clear away clouds and lurched into the news.

"The Navy seaplane, long overdue from Wake Island," he read, "has been silent for the lash eight hours." Here he turned two pages at once. "—if the President had been notivied at a nurlier dime . . ." he went on unconcernedly.

Stan grabbed the news back. "Thanks, Ray," he croaked, hardly understandable, "I think I can manage from here on."

By the heaviest effort, Stan was able to force out a whisper punctuated with capricious squeakings. He was unable to talk and was alone except for Ray, who was so thoroughly boxed that the only hope was he'd pass out and remain silent. And there were still nearly eleven of the fifteen mintes to go.

For a time they passed it back and forth, Stan struggling with his voice and Ray with his brain until Stan strode to the control room and demanded in a hysterical, squeaking whisper that they close the faders and fill with stand-by music.

One of the news writers said later that long after the interlude of music had started—long after the studio had gone dead, Ray was seated at the table, explaining with solemn inebriety that Stan's voice had given way, and that he, Ray, would bring them the news as well as messages from their sponsor.

Before we leave the matter of mishaps, two from "The Lone Ranger," one internal and the other external, so to speak, deserve note.

One night a power failure in the studio destroyed all the lights by which the actors could read, but somehow left the broadcast equipment untouched. There was confusion only for a moment. Then the cast, ad libbing as best they could, saw that some lights on the side of the building, flashing on and off, could give them enough window light to spot places in the script—perhaps even enough to read by. These lights formed a large sign which spelled "Maccabees Building." The sign came on for five seconds and was off for five. Cast members ran frantically to the windows, holding their scripts to the brief flashes of light while scanning their up-coming lines. Next they would rush back to the microphone (in the middle of the studio floor) where they delivered their lines as well as they could remember. About half the show was done in this way.

On another occasion, the Lone Ranger and Tonto were in a bad fix on the desert. Bad enough that the Lone Ranger himself was not able to travel the necessary distance to get to water and safety. Tonto resolved to set out alone in order to rush help and water back to his boss.

WXYZ in Detroit, where this show originated for many years, had then (perhaps still has) one of the most complete and realistic sound-effects departments in radio. In the studio were counters, turntables, machines, tubs. Every conceivable thing necessary to produce an authentic-sounding sound was assembled in the main studio. Some of the counters were vast panels of buttons, wired to various sound-producing devices.

In the scene where Tonto was leaving the Lone Ranger to fetch aid, the perspective stayed with the Lone Ranger, while Tonto faded into the distance. This is accomplished in radio by the actor backing away from the mike. Tonto had the ill fortune to back into and sit down on a sound truck, the top panel of which was an assortment of buttons controlling about a dozen different automobile horns.

Suddenly, in the middle of the scorching desert where, high in the shimmering heat, silent buzzards circled over bleached bones and seared cactus, the damnedest traffic jam in the history of drama materialized in a split second.

14
First Impressions

TODAY'S TV LIGHTS, except for colorcasts, are much milder than they were in the early days of television. Camera tubes of great sensitivity have replaced the older kind that had to be blasted with lights in order to produce an image. I remember newscasts in 1943 that were nightmares of heat and light. It was practically like trying to read from a paper while looking into the summer sun at noon.

Why did we try, seventeen years ago, to ignore certain facts that were obvious to the viewers? This isn't a rhetorical question, and as I write it I have no answer. I have only the question. Why did we deem it necessary, and why do some broadcasters still deem it necessary, to pretend to be comfortable when uncomfortable, cool when roasting, collected when scattered? Why did we do this when the truth was so much more interesting? Was it that clinging to a track of tradition rendered less vulnerable what we thought of as our dignity? I don't know. But I remember my first telecast.

My first telecast actually preceded my first glimpse of the medium. Preceded it by some minutes. At the time there were less than four hundred sets estimated to be in the city of Chicago—mostly in bars. I had been asked to go to WBKB to do a newscast. Arriving an hour ahead of time, a feat I have not accomplished since, I was given instructions by some sort of factotum whose position was never clear to me. The closest I can come now, in trying to figure out what he was, is the floor director, or stage manager. He gave me my news copy, which I could tell at a glance was enough for about thirty-five minutes of news. When I asked how long the newscast was to be, he told me fifteen minutes. He proceeded with pointers about reading news that made me think he believed I had had no more to do with broadcasting than a taxidermist, but I figured either he had to take a running start at the problem or he was unaware that reading news was practiced on the radio. In any case he took me into a small room that was windowless, practically without light, and so cold that I thought if I reached out in the dark I'd touch a side of beef put there for quick freezing. He flipped on a small light over the door and I could see a table and chair, a microphone, a pedestal TV camera, and my breath condensing in a pale cloud in front of my face.

"Boy, this place is chilly," I said.

"Yes," he said. "We keep the air conditioning as cold as we can." That was all the explanation I received.

Then I saw something else. I saw racks of lights—heavy spotlights such as are arranged in banks on high poles at a baseball park. They seemed to be everywhere except directly behind the chair.

At this point a young girl came in. She was wearing a fur parka with the hood thrown back. Her breath showed when she talked. As she smiled and said hello to me, my guide explained that she was the studio producer who would give me cues and timings. I knew if there was an on-the-air light and a clock, they would be all I'd need, but I kept quiet. This was television, and it might be offensive to mention radio to people in the new medium. In a way, I was right. TV has long since culled techniques from all allied media—stage, radio, and movies—adding these to its own unique methods, fusing them into a technique already bearing the first signs of a patina and soon to be burdened with the barnacles of tradition. But in those days they did things the hard way, simply because they hadn't bothered to study other media, or discover shortcuts. So I was to have cues and timings, whether I wanted them or not. And it was a good thing, because I soon found out I was not to have a clock, or an on-the-air light. The tally lights, as they are called, on the camera, are one way of telling when you are on. Two little red lights at the bottom corners of the camera come on when that camera is thrown on the program feed channel. But I got a cue from the Eskimo girl anyway.

Five minutes before air time she offered to take my jacket, pointing out that there was nowhere to hang it on walls which were entirely covered by banks of lights.

I told her I'd keep my coat, but thanks anyway. She shrugged and donned a one-eared headset such as is worn by telephone operators. The headset had a little transmitter-microphone on a curved metal rod that brought it close to her mouth. She spoke into this, presumably to the control room, asking for a timing. There were three and a half minutes to go. A test pattern, up on a rack on casters, was moved noisily out of the room. Later I learned that the camera had to be scanned, and that this was the purpose of a test pattern. Remember when they used to broadcast test patterns for what seemed like hours a day? That was so you could scan your TV set, and make sure that a circle was circular and a square was square and that one-hundred-and-ten pound girls five-feet-one didn't come across looking like one-hundred-eighty-five pound girls three-feet-two. Do you want to know why they don't do that any more? There are two reasons. One is that sets are made better today and are less apt to distort, the other is that they've found it doesn't hurt the rating of a show if ninety-pound girls six feet tall come over as three-hundred-pound girls *one* foot tall.

At a minute to go, as I sat there shivering, my nose red and my lips blue, my hands and feet numb and my blood congealed, the Eskimo girl removed her parka, under which she had a halter and shorts that looked more like a swim suit. And in tones of portent, as if she were John Daly asking Time itself to come in and sign in please, she said, "One minute!" dropped her parka in a corner and faced me with one hand on a well-shaped hip and the other half-raised. I couldn't decide whether she intended to do an interpretive dance behind my chair as I read the news, was thus clad to inspire or divert me, or wanted to make me feel ashamed of complaining about the cold by chattering my teeth.

"Lights!" she shouted. The banks came on, one by one, in five-second intervals.

The first bank was ahead of me and slightly to the left. It had perhaps fifteen spots of impressive wattage which bore down on me, my little table and my papers with an actual, palpable thrust. The second bank came on—ahead and to the right. It was like fifteen more suns, bearing down in a way that made me understand how those little paddle things in jewelers' windows are made to revolve by the actual force of light. I thought if I lifted a sheet of my news broadside to that light, it would be blasted away.

It pained me now to look at the papers. I had narrowed my eyes to squinty slits through which that torrent of light smashed its way to my aching retinas.

To my right another bank of light came on. I narrowed my eyes further and finally shut one of them completely. We are endowed with two eyes for many reasons. One of them is that we can still see enough to navigate by looking through one eye while we spare the other from destruction. I suddenly realized I wasn't cold any more.

Finally the last bank of lights came on at my left.

The obvious reason for not throwing this entire inferno into play at once was that every master fuse in the city would have blown out, plunging Chicago into a blackout. Subways would have been darkened and stopped in their tubes. Hospitals would have gone suddenly on their emergency battery systems, millions of ice cubes would have started to melt in refrigerators as far south as Cicero, and people in elevators would have panicked in the silent dark between floors.

I had never seen light like this in my life. I have never seen it since. Yet I have squinted against giant sun reflectors in making movies. I have been on color telecasts where the light requirements are roughly eight times as heavy as for present-day black and white television shows. I have looked, momentarily, on the face of the sun itself. Never have I felt such sheer withering force of light as I felt during that tormented quarter-hour. Within seconds my irises had clanked down to pinhole size. Still the light roared in through my eyelids, so that I could see traces of veins in them. I tried to keep my hands away, because if I once covered my eyes I might never have had the courage to uncover them.

My female director, who must have been standing beside the camera, started a countdown. I was relieved, although surprised, to hear her voice, and to know she was still alive. For although I was at the focal point of that blazing fulgence, she was nearer some of the banks. I was afraid to inhale for fear I'd smell burning flesh.

As the countdown proceeded, many thoughts spread through my mind: I should have taken my coat off as I was told. I had to get my eyes open somehow and look into the camera and say some sort of greeting. I had fifteen minutes to endure somehow, unless a power failure saved me. Were all television cameras this hungry for illumination of their subjects? Or did this one have no picture tube, being designed to have the lens focus an image on the end of the cable and send it out direct?

"Five, four, three, two—" she went on, and still my eyes were shut.

"One," she finished. I suppose she waved her arm on zero instead of saying "Fire!" I was sorry she didn't say "Fire!" because it would have been excuse enough for me to barrel out of the place saying "Fire!" myself and maybe, "Save the women!"

We get used to anything. While I said my opening words into the camera with my eyes still tight shut, looking, I suppose, as if I were praying, or in agony, or both, I gradually cracked one and then the other eye open and read through the only quarter-hour of TV news that was a full hour and a half long to the newscaster.

Within five minutes, perspiration was dripping from the end of my nose and chin. I ignored it. After ten minutes my shirt and tie were soaked and water was seeping through my jacket. Which was a good thing, since it cut down the likelihood of my clothing catching fire.

When I finished the last line of news and croaked out a sign-off with parched throat and slightly swollen tongue, I was two pounds lighter.

Before the camera tally lights had dropped the spotlights went out, and within twenty seconds the temperature was on its way back down to thirty degrees Absolute.

I sat there for a moment in the relative darkness of an ordinary three-hundred-watt bulb, unable to move.

The Eskimo's voice came cheerily to me. "You'd better not sit there long. You've been perspiring!"

"Yeah. I know." I said weakly. "And it'll freeze on me. How do you stand it?"

"You get used to it," she laughed.

"I doubt if I will. I think I'll stick to radio," I muttered.

15
Catastrophes and Stiff Upper Lips

IT WOULD SEEM that the chances for "goofs" in TV might be less than in radio since so many more people are involved. The margin for error would, of course, increase with the number of people involved, but the compound error that makes a video goof, it would seem, should be less, where there are so many steps in which to correct a situation before it gets on the air. However, they happen.

Examples of two relatively recent calamities occurred on the Paar show and the old Home show. In demonstrating a flea and tick killer for dogs, which is sprayed from an aerosol can, I rehearsed in the studio before air time, spraying out and slightly to the side, so the spray would show up. It worked fine. On the air, all conditions were identical, except that with an audience present in the theater, the air conditioning was boosted slightly. Just enough that the cloud of flea killer hung for a moment in suspension, and then drifted back on me as I continued my spiel. Retribution visited me in the same manner that armies in World War I were embarrassed to find the poison-gas clouds returning after a shift of wind. For a few seconds I ignored it, but when it gripped my throat with scratchy claws, I coughed, and from there on the commercial was a shambles. I fell apart laughing, explained to the audience what had happened, and gave up, expecting NBC would have to rebate the cost of the commercial. It happens the client—I may as well tell you, since such things are certainly no secret—Sergeant's Dog Care Products, took a light-hearted view of it. The incident caused considerable comment, and we learned later that sales resulting from their campaign ran some three hundred per cent higher than had been estimated.

Two or three years before that, the chef on the Home show found himself in a predicament entailing a type of discomfort that makes me shudder to think about it.

He demonstrated how to make taffy and pull it by hand. If you think you've guessed the end of this story, you're right. But how could such a thing happen? He had rehearsed carefully; he knew with the knowledge of the expert, just how the taffy should be prepared. The slip-up was something he could not possibly control. The lighting director watched the rehearsal, frowned slightly, consulted the video shading engineer, then ordered two thousand watts of light added to the area.

Now the chef was working in a narrow margin. With the taffy too cool, he could not possibly work it to the state he desired in the time he had. With it too warm, all the butter and skill in the world could not keep it from bonding to his skin. He had it figured down to the precise degree and was, of course, done in by the heat added when that Klieg light was aimed at him.

It may be second guessing or even my imagination, now that I look back on that scene, but I fancy that after he'd been on a minute and a half, he cast one worried glance at the beam that hadn't been there when he went through it for cameras earlier. He sensed that something was wrong, with that sixth sense that can issue a vague warning of impending ruin, yet still not spell it out.

"Now you must be sure," he was saying, "that you put plenty of butter on your hands." He put plenty on. More, I thought, than he had used in the rehearsal. "Because you know what can happen if this stuff once gets hold of you." Although he smiled here, there was in that smile a whiff of sickness. It was the smile of a man speaking to his seconds under the oaks, just before a duel which he hadn't wanted in the first place. The chef started to pull. All went well the first three or four passes and then he made a sudden frantic motion, freeing himself from a small tentacle that had lashed out and fused to his wrist right at the base of the palm. Putting the whole gob down, he quickly went to the butter tray and applied butter again lavishly to both hands and halfway up his arms. He resumed the struggle, saying nothing. Beads of perspiration appeared on his forehead. A strange silence gripped the studio—stagehands, cable men, carpenters, special effects people, even maintenance personnel began to crowd into the cooking area with morbid fascination. They stayed out of camera, but they were hovering, powerless either to help the chef or to turn their eyes from what we all knew at this point was certain disaster.

As he shifted the taffy for a new pull we saw that some of it had oozed between the index and middle fingers of his right hand. He made a sudden stab at the butter with his left hand and pried himself loose. His next sentence showed his awareness of his plight. It was laden with doom. "It's hot in here," he said. Gordon Wayne, the stage manager, slipped out to rouse the building engineers for more air conditioning, although he must have known they couldn't have acted fast enough to save the chef.

Now it had him in two places on the left hand. In trying to free himself he involved his right hand. It was in a twisted position when the thing caught him and in straightening it, he wrapped it nearly all the way around his hand. From this moment on he was doomed. An audible groan went up along with several snickers.

In desperation, the chef suddenly adopted a jolly mood. Chuckling, he said something to the effect that he had somehow done the very thing he'd been cautioning everyone against. He started to lurch off in the direction of explaining that he had done this deliberately to illustrate as dramatically as possible how terrible this sort of thing could be, but it lacked conviction and he abandoned it in midstream. With it he abandoned his jolly mood and gave way to sheer terror.

The taffy was now not only firmly welded to the skin of his hands and arms, but his struggling had pressed it against his apron and shirt. There was, in the nature of his convulsions, a hint that he regarded this as some living, evil thing. Unable now to do anything with his hands, he started biting at it, thereby not only gluing it to his face, but closing his jaws. His last words were "Well, it *tastes* good anyway."

He had to be rescued. The rescuers were understandably hesitant. I think if the chef had been down under a high-tension wire we'd have gone to his aid more fearlessly. Somehow the prospect of being engulfed, possibly assimilated, by that shapeless, stringy horror, made the stoutest hearts quail.

Taffy is, however, water-soluble, so I'm able to report that today the chef is alive and well and heads a fancy international restaurant at the largest airport in the world.

In those same days before methods were borrowed from older, simpler stage traditions, some studios had not yet learned that a prop need not be the real thing. If, in a TV or dramatic production, the script calls for a real chair, it is obvious that a real chair will be the cheapest, easiest way of fulfilling the requirement. But if the script should call for a bottle of vintage wine, there is no reason for using the real thing in the drama, and, indeed, there are excellent reasons for using a substitute. Diluted grape juice or Kool-Aid will do the job better.

An old Chicago actor ran afoul of this difficulty once in a dramatic bit on an early TV station. The script called for the character he portrayed to snatch up a bottle of formaldehyde, pull a lusty swig from it, and then fall down on the floor announcing in agony that he was perishing, as one very likely would be after such folly.

This luckless thespian very nearly played his role to a realistic end. Up through dress rehearsal there were some props missing, and he had been using an empty bottle. The prop man, on going over the list, saw the item Bottle of Formaldehyde. This was, of course, not to be a practical prop. In theater, a prop may or may not be practical. For example, a lamp in a living room may never be plugged in if it is never to be turned on in the course of the play. It may not even have a cord or a bulb. This is a prop that is not practical. If it is to be turned on or off during the drama, then it is indicated on the prop man's sheet as practical. In the case of a bottle of such potent stuff as formaldehyde, I doubt if any theater prop man in his right mind would take it to be practical in anything but a science show—certainly not in a drama. If it were listed as practical, he would probably question it, checking with the director as to whether he was to get a real bottle of the stuff. Otherwise his job is to fill a bottle with liquid, probably water, and affix a realistic Formaldehyde label.

This dolt, as you've undoubtedly guessed, procured and put on the shelf of the set a real bottle of formaldehyde. Fortunately the poor actor merely touched it to his lips, but it began immediately to embalm the top end of his alimentary tract, and when, on the floor, he began to shriek that he was dying, he thought he was. The other actors were impressed at first by the thoroughness of his suddenly inspired acting, and then annoyed by his obvious upstaging tactics of continuing with his lines, padding his part beyond recognition.

"I'm really dying," he choked. "I'm not acting! Get me to a hospital!" They finally got the idea. Doctors were summoned and he was sped to Wesley Memorial in an ambulance. He recovered.

"Hawkins Falls," a well-written and well-produced soap opera, was for some years sponsored by a leading detergent. I was the announcer on that dramatic serial, out of Chicago. After beginning and ending commercials, I closed the show with what's called "voice-over" copy—that is, I was not seen, but I read closing copy while the picture on the TV screen was of the town of Hawkins Falls along with screen credits.

Jim Troy, now a successful producer, was then stage manager for Hawkins Falls. In Chicago, the stage manager was called the floor director. He really ran things from the floor, having the responsibility of seeing that certain pictures, mechanical devices and people were in place on time. In addition, he gave cues, and speed-ups and slow-downs. It's a busy job. Jim did it with enough efficiency that he knew when he was not needed and could stay out of the way. In fact, once that show "shook down," there were vast stretches during which he could stay away long enough to get a nap, if it had been a hard day.

Many of the props were stored for short periods right in the studio, but in a corner away from the sets. This was particularly true of props that might be used again in a day or so. One of our favorite props was a hammock that was set up from time to time in the back yard of a house in Hawkins Falls, but when that set wasn't in play, the hammock stayed backstage where it tempted any of us who, feeling the need of relaxation, could get to it first. Since it was the kind of hammock that has its own metal frame, no trees were necessary. It was strung all the time.

One day, near the end of the show, things were going smoothly, and Jim got to the hammock. I couldn't have used it just then because I had some voice-over copy to read. For this, since I wasn't seen on camera, I wore a headset of my own. As a result, I could take my cue directly from the control room. I could also hear everything that was said in control to the cameramen and to Jim.

Piled on the foot end of the hammock were about a dozen grass mats, whose naps are indistinguishable from grass on television. If you have a scene where you must shoot the ground or a portion of lawn, you cover the studio floor in the area with grass mats. Jim, preparing to lie in the hammock, sat on the head end. His weight carried him down and raised the foot end of the hammock nine feet into the air, grass mats and all. This event occurred just as I started to read my voice-over copy. Out of the corner of my eye I saw the hammock rear up like an angry horse, depositing Jim on the floor and then the grass mats on Jim. After the hammock clanked back into position, I could see a struggling green mound near it. Jim was trying desperately to extricate himself from the ersatz lawn that had enveloped him. The whole thing looked like an animated grave on its way to an appearance on "What's My Line?"

I might have avoided breaking up if it hadn't been for what I heard from the control room: the director's voice saying, "Can't you keep 'em quiet down there, Jim?"

Hawkins Falls had no audio end that day except for theme music. Had my mike been left open, there'd have been nothing audible but a wheezing, helpless, depraved and mirth-rooted fit.

16
The Ad Game

"Our fluent men of place and consequence
Fumble and fill their mouths with hollow phrase,
Or for the end-all of deep arguments
Intone their dull commercial liturgies."

W<small>HEN</small> William Vaughn Moody wrote these lines there was no radio or television, but his inadvertent prophecy points up the prominence given to personalities in broadcasting who use their personalities to influence the buying habits of masses of people who tune them in.

"A picture is worth a thousand words" is a cliché which was much used in the early days of television by salesmen who tried to get clients to take radio advertising money out of radio and put it into television. The saying comes from an old Chinese proverb that translates, "One picture is worth more than ten thousand words"—a little stronger.

The first commercial I saw on television I will remember always, because it actually made me hungry. A boy opened a bag of potato chips on the screen. Just two senses operative here—the sight of fresh potato chips and the sound of the bag being opened and a chip being crunched. No smell, no taste or touch, and no words from anyone—at least not then. If I had been hungry before I was not aware of it, but it made me hungry. It was a better institutional commercial than brand commercial, inasmuch as I wasn't persuaded that all other brands were inferior, and I can't even remember now which brand was being lauded. Nevertheless, the ability to appeal to an appetite via the senses of sight and sound (which is television) impressed me tremendously.

A *Newsweek* article during the quiz investigations called TV "... an industry which confuses the illusion of art with the trickery of the huckster...." This statement is a broad one. The truth is that a part of the industry cunningly employs the illusions of visual arts for huckster trickery, and another part struggles to preserve integrity and to keep faith with the public by opposing such tactics.

One of the reactions to investigation of commercials was the suppression of legitimate theatrical techniques in conveying truths about a product.

A case in point involves a paint-plaster whose commercial message demonstrated how it fills cracks and holes in plaster walls. It was discovered that when a section of a cracked wall is set before a television camera, the cracks do not show except in extreme close-ups. The agency conceived the idea of running a lead pencil along the cracks in order to make them show up. This suggestion was made to me with some question as to whether I would go along with it. It was felt I might regard the penciling as fraud. Clearly, the doubt must have come from a failure to understand the nature of fraud. The pencil marks do not help the product to fill the cracks—they merely allow the viewers to see what's being filled. Had the agency or client come to me and said, "Our product does not fill cracks very well. Therefore in order to make a foolproof demonstration we wish to leave the plaster uncracked, and pencil in fake crack lines," then of course I would have had nothing to do with it. That is fraud. Advertising of that type (and it's undeniable that there has been some) should be forced off the air.

Advertising calls public attention to something in such a way as to emphasize its desirable qualities and to increase its sale. Advertising must have started in primitive communities as soon as there was more than one source of the same product or service.

Let us suppose that in a tribe that drifted between the Pyrenees and the middle regions of France about 35,000 years ago, one Ooku, flintwright, had had a virtual monopoly on arrowheads, spearheads, and axheads. He had never bothered to tell anyone how good his products were—they spoke for themselves. None of the rest of the warriors and hunters of the tribe could chip flint as skillfully or quickly as Ooku. In fact Ooku had quit hunting and fighting when he was still a young man and had devoted the last eighteen years to making flint tips for weapons. When men wanted his products, they brought him such things as he deemed acceptable in exchange. The choicest grubs, nuts, berries, medicinal herbs and roots, the finest fresh meat and aged marrow, the highest quality cured skins and furs were his in trade for his excellent products. He even had some interior decorating done on his cave one spring. A young artist had come from as far away as Altamira, Spain (known up to then only as the land beyond the mountains), and painted a buffalo on one of the smooth walls. This was in payment for half a dozen arrowheads and a pelt scraper.

Ooku, in short, had it made. His fame, and the tribe's

admiration for his skill, put him in the most elevated social group. His children had individual tutoring from the highest-paid teachers in javelin throwing and in-fighting, and his wife, who had never worn anything but furs, now sported a genuine cloth coat from a northern tribe which practiced the art of weaving.

Suddenly, business began to slow up. Ooku had no idea why until one of his customers said, "I'm sorry, Ooku, but Glung will give me this size spearhead for half as much honey."

"Glung?" said Ooku, his eyes narrowing. "Who's this Glung?"

"He's a young guy who winters at the fork of the stream. He's just about given up hunting, because he chips flint pretty good and the hunters bring him food in exchange for his stuff. I'm sorry. I've been trading with you for a long time, Ooku, but honey's hard to get, what with getting stung all the time, and I have to make it go as far as I can. If Glung offers me a better deal, I'll have to get my arrowheads from him. I hope you understand."

Ooku understood, all right. Someone had moved in on his racket. The solution was simple. He would lash one of his own spearheads to a shaft and go over to the fork of the stream and drive the whole thing squarely through Glung's middle, and then everything would be as it was.

But would it? Glung's relatives might lash one of Glung's spearheads to a shaft and push it through Ooku's middle. And even if they didn't, the Chief might have a counsel with the old men of the tribe, and they'd come forth with some kind of nonsense about Glung's having as much right to live and develop a skill as anyone else. He was in the soup, any way he turned.

He moped for several days.

His wife, coming in one afternoon in her cloth coat,

asked him why he was moping. He explained the situation to her.

"Why don't you make some little improvement in your flints," she suggested, "and then tell everybody they're better than Glung's? It won't get all your customers back, but at least you won't lose them all."

"What do you mean 'tell everybody'?"

"Go out and holler how your flints are improved, and how long you've been making quality products. How yours are worth the extra loot."

Ooku did better than that. He hired a neighbor to go around the tribe hollering about the excellence of Ooku's New Improved Arrowheads. The improvement was a deeper nock at the back of the head to allow more thong in the binding. Ooku's wife said it didn't matter whether it was a real improvement or not, it was a good gimmick to hang a campaign on.

So product advertising was born.

The neighbor who did Ooku's commercials had a few wrinkles up his sleeve too. He went to the fellow with the honey (who might be moved in on at any moment by a younger honey-hunter) and made a deal to cry *his* product among tribe members. After awhile he got several other accounts and farmed out some of the commercials to his kids.

And so the ad agency was born.

Probably advertising is older than this. It may have involved services before it did products. It also probably outdates spoken language. The first nonverbal communication on the part of a seductive woman promising something in return for something else was a commercial—a very durable one which has undergone little alteration in eons of time.

Advertising is just about as necessary as production to make a product succeed. So advertising is a fact of life. And as long as you and I and hundreds of millions of others continue to buy things, we will continue to run into commercial messages telling us what things to buy and why—messages staring at us from our magazines, interrupting our television shows, lining the insides of our public conveyances, jumping out at us from roadside signs, tucked in between every two musical selections our car radios bring us.

An intelligent buyer will neither swallow all this fodder nor shut it out completely. Advertising is educational even though it is not impartial. (Suppose product A *is* better than product B. It could be. Give it a try.)

Commercials represent the best efforts a company and its advertising agency can put forth in bidding for your patronage. In broadcasting there is quite a range from the simple inexpensive announcement on a small radio station to the production commercial in a TV spectacular.

In a minimal spot announcement on local radio there may be three people involved—a man who sells the spot and reads it himself on the air after writing it, the advertising man at the company who buys the time, and the transmitter engineer. The equipment involved is a typewriter, a microphone and studio amplification equipment, and the transmitter and tower. The cost for the announcement might be twenty dollars.

Contrast this with the other extreme. The most elaborate and expensive commercial I have ever known was produced for the Ford Motor Company to introduce the 1958 Ford. It was filmed, and it was aired once. It involved Arthur Godfrey, Dick Powell, myself as spokesman, roughly thirty models and extras, a production agency and an ad agency, two film companies, fifteen automobiles, special effects, sound, set designers, stagehands, editors, caterers, a composer and arranger and full symphonic-size orchestra. In addition there was the personnel at the network centers (New York and Hollywood) where the commercial was run simultaneously in a total of four projectors in case of mechanical or cable failure. It was made over a period of a month and a half in three states, using three film studios (two Manhattan sound stages and one in Los Angeles), two tape studios and an armory in New Jersey, because one sequence involved a turning model of the earth too large to fit in any sound stage in the world. It cost over a quarter of a million dollars. Many handsome radio stations are available lock, stock and barrel for less money than that single commercial.

Human emotion is a priceless thing. Elation and agony are simply not proportionate to the money involved in a triumph or a disaster. When a commercial, for example, is mishandled or in some way destroyed, the distress of those involved in the debacle has nothing to do with how costly the spot may have been. I have been acutely distressed over bungling a $150 radio spot, and relatively calm about an $8000 one going down the spout. I put one a little more costly than that in the hands of a female guest once and watched with something like detachment while it disintegrated before my eyes.

Disorder and heartbreak once resulted from an incident a friend of mine was later able to laugh about. Ken Griffin, one of the best romantic leads in radio strip serials (he was Dr. Brent in "Road of Life" and Larry Noble in "Backstage Wife" for years), once worked as announcer in a small station in the South. His boss, the program director of the station, had sold a spot to a local manufacturer of overalls—special overalls for field hands picking cotton. He had written the copy himself and rushed it in to Ken who was on duty with instructions to read it on the air as soon as possible. Ken said he'd read it at the end of the recorded selection currently playing. The program director said that was not soon enough—he was to fade the music and read it instantly. Ken shrugged and faded the music.

Another announcer was in the booth with him at the time. Ken had no time to glance over the copy. Two big selling points of these garments were an extra thickness of cloth in the seat and a button arrangement on the trouser cuffs which shut out dust.

Ken launched into it on the air, cold. "Friends," he started, "Midland now offers overalls to men with double seats." He stopped a moment, and in the silence the other announcer snorted audibly. Ken fought the laughter crowding into his throat, got control and took a running start from the beginning.

"Friends, Midland now offers overalls to men with double seats, with button bottoms . . ."

That was the end of the announcement. Both of them were fired on the spot.

Another friend of mine worked on a small station in Michigan where the local concern that bottled Seven-Up also handled a drink called Squirt. The station announcers thought they were doing the client and the salesman a favor when they altered the copy to read "Drink Squirt and Seven-Up." The salesman asked them to read it as originally written, which was, "Drink Seven-Up and Squirt." The boys had trouble getting through it and thought the salesman was crazy. I think he was smart enough to belong right then on Madison Avenue in an office with a thick rug. It was the talk of the town. And a lot of Seven-Up and Squirt were sold.

Madison Avenue has had much recent publicity, mostly in the form of daring exposés. An exposé is only daring if what it exposes is sinister and in some way a danger even to the *exposer*. I don't think many of the authors of these works felt they could be hurt in writing what they did. Even those who knew they cut their cables behind them were not the targets of organized retribution from the agency world. Ironically, the machinery of Madison Avenue grinds along with almost no emotion—it is so totally expedient that those clever enough to write such persuasive propaganda about the ad business would be welcomed back, for the most part, as idea men at rather high figures—in at least one case this happened, I understand.

Is Madison Avenue a sinister force in our lives? Do the ad men cheat consumers of goods, the readers of magazines and viewers of TV shows choking with commercials? Are we being robbed to support this fantastic machinery? Don't we really pay for the advertising in the long run, inasmuch as the products could be sold at a lower price if advertising did not exist?

My answer to the first question is No. The major threat to our way of life is probably a political state of affairs wherein advertising could not exist because the government would control all produce. In that case, free enterprise would be dead. To the second question I say No. We aren't being robbed. We are willingly paying the price in order to buy the advertised item. It is true that we pay for advertising in the long run. But we have proved millions of times that we encourage the system.

If, starting tomorrow, a sizable majority of people bought the most of those things that were advertised the least, and continued to show allegiance to those companies that bothered us least with commercials, advertising as a business would collapse in a decade. We the people are responsible for the existence of agencies that make millions telling companies how to tell us why we should buy their stuff.

A. C. Spectorsky, in his book *The Exurbanites*, refers to those who work in advertising as "symbol manipulators" as opposed to people who are "thing manipulators." Men who run factories for canning vegetables are thing manipulators. Not only the fellow who puts the vegetables in the can itself, but the president of the canning company—all of them are thing manipulators. Those who work with opinion and devise ways to get the public to purchase this or that particular brand of canned vegetables are symbol manipulators.

There seem to be certain characteristics of symbol manipulators, setting them apart from folks in any other walk of life. Although these characteristics do not mark all or even a majority of those engaged in the advertising business, enough of them are so marked to provide a recognizable syndrome, and to have hatched a biased view of all ad agency personnel.

I refer to a soulless expediency that frequently renders the agency man arrogant with those he considers to have less status than himself, while remaining unabashedly obsequious to those of higher status. Unlike the martinet, however, who behaves thus with passion, our ad agency specimen pursues this path, as he pursues everything, without passion, maintaining a humorless and reptilian alertness. He often gives the impression that stabbed, he would seep ichor instead of blood.

And this alien mettle invades every department of his

life. He will dress as he is told, drink what he is supposed to, live where he should, and take his headaches home with him on the suburban train. He will calculate the value of favors received and bestowed, drop friendships that get in the way of his Steps Forward, anesthetize sets of values that make his methods seem awkward, and sell out his store of loyalty and love in a spiritual bankruptcy beside which any folly of the flesh is paltry.

The books that paint this picture have not exaggerated; they have distorted the state of things with the implication that the disease is more widespread than it actually is. But it exists. And the most curious and appalling thing about it is that, although it exists in many other professions and businesses, it is characterized there by stealth. In advertising alone it is enough out in the open to shed a strange light on the whole industry. It is as though the habit of manipulating human opinion tends to make the manipulators feel that self-opinions are pliable enough to be worthless. Opinion of themselves is therefore not important to them.

This is true of most dedicated people. And this type of ad agency man is dedicated.

A commercial on NBC television once required a ball to be dropped into a funnel while an announcer read copy presumably written to time out right. The ball kept coming through the funnel sooner than desired. Several remedies were suggested by the director and property man, ranging from altering the design of the funnel, to shortening the copy. Nothing could be changed without consultation on a higher level than the agency man could arrange at the moment. At length he decided the thing to do was to have the stagehand drop the ball *more slowly*. He did not mean, it developed, for the stagehand to delay dropping the ball, nor to raise its starting point. He meant what he said, and when he repeated it his voice carried the clear implication that it was The Client who wanted it this way. If certain physical laws of the universe stood in the way of success, the universe had better look out.

A powerful newspaper publisher in Chicago once planned to attend a showing of some film footage taken on his estate to be used as promotional advertising for his newspaper. It included a great Dane of which he was very proud. He announced that he and the dog would be present in the viewing room at 2:00 PM sharp. His agency was instructed to roll the film at 2:00 PM sharp. The strict wording of the order left no doubt that there should, under no circumstances, be a delay.

At three minutes of two the publisher's great Dane arrived in the company of a trainer. The publisher was not with them. At 2:00 PM sharp, still no publisher. The agency contingent held a hurried meeting and made a decision. They rolled the film for the dog. The publisher failed completely to show, but his orders were carried out by an agency as faithful as it was humorless.

Most of the harsh comment on ad agencies has been written in the false judgment of bitterness. Rancor always works from a narrow perspective. The specifics are true, but the criticism fails, as a rule, to embody the reasons for things being as they are.

If ever there was a middleman, it is the ad agency. It stands between the arts and the purse strings. It is the buffer between creative pride and mercantile ruthlessness. And it gets bruised on both sides. It may well be the most pressured business in the world, constantly trying to effect a marriage of incompatible outlooks, or at least to keep peace between them. It incurs the disfavor of both factions.

I believe if all ad agencies closed for one month, and let business concerns work out their advertising problems directly with media, that at the end of that time, both media and the corporations would be so glad to see the agencies back that loud rejoicing would break forth. Maybe even a book or two would appear in praise of Madison Avenue.

17
Our Daily Bread

THE LAST COUPLE of years have been busy ones for me not only because of a heavy broadcasting schedule, but because of other interests I pursue. I have been asked by many people, at various times, what my life is like and what kind of a daily routine I follow.

To begin with, there is no such thing as a typical day in the life of a broadcaster. Every day is different from every other day. Some are as average as a bus driver's or a dentist's, and others leave me in a state of shock at bedtime—wondering how it all happened, and in some cases, even if it did really happen.

The first alarm (electric) sounded at 7:32 and the second (wind-up) at 7:35. I had set the clocks early because I'd promised my son I'd look at a homework problem of his, and this was the only chance I'd have to do it.

The electric alarm produces a highly offensive nasal buzz that won't unwind or weaken unless the city power fails. Since electric power does fail occasionally, I also have the wind-up alarm. This one emits a clatter calculated by a genius of industrial design to encompass in one bell-sound the effect of a heavily laden milkman toppling over among empty garbage pails at the same instant that a large bank's burglar alarm cuts loose. It is most effective.

I heard the first alarm's buzz as though it were faded in by a skilled audio engineer. The level was brought up slowly out of nowhere, in the manner of a person who eases up behind you, so that when you do become aware of his presence you are also aware that he has been there for some time. This makes the discovery more shocking than a frank and noisy approach would have been. When I did really hear that brash buzz it triggered the first phase of my awakening—clear-eyed alertness—a terror flavored with resentment.

I sat bolt upright, with no idea where I was, nor what time of the day or what day of the week it was. I asked Ruth what we were doing in a Paris railroad station. Which got no response whatever, even when I poked at her, since she was in another part of the apartment, having got up a half hour before. I sat up straighter, and my panic began to fade into a stupor, which always threatens my balance unless I act quickly. It was this quick action that deposited me on the floor. I swung my feet down to join the rest of me and began a rise to a full stand. Naturally I was not going to *execute* a full stand, because I would have fallen flat on my face. That lacks dignity and makes a loud noise. It's better to let the knees buckle gradually, and, keeping the back against the lower sheet (sometimes called the under sheet or standing rigging of the bed), allow the weight of the body to work against the friction of the bedclothes, and thus lower oneself to the floor.

After a little practice, this results in a motion that embodies considerable grace.

From my new vantage point, both clocks could be silenced. Now the first thoughts of the day began to take form.

What's my name?

Why did I dream we should suspend diplomatic relations with Easthampton, Long Island?

Should we suspend diplomatic relations with Easthampton, Long Island?

When Frank Sinatra was a little boy, there were probably very few people who wanted his autograph.

My right foot is still asleep.

In New Zealand at this very moment, theater curtains are coming down and people are going home to go to bed.

I could say I thought I was a New Zealander and that's why I didn't show up for work today.

This is very comfortable, but I really should try to get up.

At this point, I reached out and shut off the electric alarm. For the next five seconds or so I stared at it without thinking and without breathing. Then I resumed breathing, and let my eyes go the rest of the way shut, which wasn't very far. More thoughts began to take shape:

It's a lovely time of year.

What is?

This time of year.

Do you know what time of year this time of year is?

No.

I thought so.

It's winter and there's nothing but ankle-high slush outside, along with air that has a lot of soot in it.

I don't give a damn.

Go ahead and don't.

Do horses know they are divided into withers and gaskins and fetlocks, or do they just think they are all horse?

That other alarm may go off any minute—any second now.

I am not going to be taken by surprise.

How do you know your grocer doesn't carry a concealed weapon?

When I look in that mirror in the bathroom—and I must soon—I shall remind myself again that I am sixteen years younger than Cary Grant.

If Zsa Zsa Gabor had been born a quarter of a century later in Boone, Iowa, she would be out selling girl scout cookies this very minute.

Shut off the other alarm and get to your feet.

No, if I sit here awhile longer everything will go away and I will be happy.

Here consciousness faded, giving the illusion that everything had gone away. I was happy. Almost euphoric. Then I was taken by surprise. A heavily laden milkman toppled forward among empty garbage pails at the same instant that a large bank's burglar alarm cut loose.

I must get to my feet. They need me out there.

That's the alarm, you idiot.

Get it turned off before it wakes the baby.

You haven't had a baby in the house for ten years.

Well, before it wakes the neighborhood, then.

One eye came open enough for me to get a fix on the clock. I made a motion with my right arm which knocked it off the stand.

Now you must stand on your feet.

Nothing hasty.

Yes. Something hasty. It is 7:35 and you promised you'd help him.

I struggled to a standing position, weaving a bit.

If your center of gravity, which is between the solar plexus and the spine, but in your case, getting lower every year in spite of your fat head, doesn't hang out over your base, which is your feet and plenty big, you will remain balanced in an upright position. If this condition isn't met you will go over like a giant Douglas fir.

And no one will be sorry.

I started to walk. After two tentative steps I stopped to stretch. This was quite satisfying, but had the effect, as it always does, of throwing me off course enough to walk square into the wall. I woke up a little more, uncorked some unprintable invectives about the design of my bedroom, and fumbled my way into the bathroom.

As I turned on the tap I peered into the glass on the door of the medicine chest.

"I am sixteen years older than Charles Coburn," I muttered.

The sound of my voice startled me and must have startled Ruth, too.

"Are you talking to yourself?" she called.

"No," I said, more loudly and in a thick voice.

"You're talking to yourself," she asserted, "and when you talk to yourself you aren't awake."

"I'm not talking to myself," I said. "I'm thinking out loud. There's a difference."

By the time I'd put cold water on my face I began to function. I knew who I was, and what day of the week it was, and had in mind the next steps in the process of getting dressed. Shaving went rapidly and smoothly, and after three minutes in a cool shower I knew every facet of the day, including the immediate homework promise to my son.

H.R. had eaten breakfast and was at his desk when I went into his room.

"Hi," he said. "I thought maybe I could figure it out before you came in, but I can't. Look at this."

I looked at it. It was a question in a review test, and it didn't look too involved. Fortunately, his school problems are, for the most part, still in my scope. I have about another year and then I'm through. I never hesitate to say "I don't know" when I don't, but it's embarrassing to have to do that with simple fractions, which I never learned. And it will be embarrassing to have to do it with every feature of every subject he studies next year. I can sense it coming.

"Well," I said in a tone that conveyed enough paternal solicitude to inspire the security that comes to a child when he thinks his parents are wise, "you have here a fairly complex problem. But not complex in depth. Only laterally. I might say the complexity is more an aggregation of drudging details than anything formidable in the way of logical intricacy."

He looked at me and blinked. "I think anyone knows *that*," he said. "What I need help with—"

"I don't want to hand you the answer. I've told you that before. There's no real help to you if I do the work *for* you, but only if—"

"I'll say," he interrupted. "It's too often wrong."

"Now that'll be enough of *that*," I said firmly, but without rancor.

"All right, don't get sore," he placated. "Just show me how to get the right answer to the last part. Please..."

I sighed and plunged into it.

He worked away in that almost unreadable scrawl of his, and presently sat looking at me and tapping his pencil resonantly on his skull while I multiplied.

"Stuck, huh?" I said as I wrote out my answer.

"No, I finished it."

"What did you get?"

"20256 square feet."

"Well, you're all right except for the middle digit. It's 20156 square feet. That's what you can get for hurrying. If you're off a hundred square feet—for that matter if you're off *one* square foot, you might as well be off a thousand, because they'll count it wrong—"

"Mine's right," he said, matter-of-factly. "You forgot to carry one after the six and nine is fifteen."

He was right. Even fathers can be fallible, and that in itself is an important lesson in the life of the older child. We had a good laugh, and I resisted the impulse to knock the smirk off his face with a right cross.

Together we subtracted, added, divided, and multiplied. At each step H.R. came out ahead of me and waited, tapping his pencil.

At one of the steps I multiplied by .333 to get one-third of a quantity. Before I'd finished he announced, "5998 square feet."

"That's pretty close," I said. "I've got 5992.335—"

"Why didn't you take a third instead of multiplying by a decimal?" he asked.

I looked at him for a silent moment. "You know I never learned to do fractions," I said.

"You wouldn't need to. You could just divide by three."

How could the kid be so tactless? The Truth, delivered without some cushioning wrap of hypocrisy, is tactlessness. Add forthright and dead right and you get tactless. He merely pointed out the truth. Then it dawned on me.

"If you got the right answer this easily, why did you want me to get up early to help you with it? You said you were stuck."

"I am."

"How?"

"Well, the rest of the problem. I have to list the steps I took to get the answer."

"Why, then," I raised my voice patiently, "did you have me go through this whole problem if you already had done it and had the right answer?"

"That was your idea, not mine."

He went off to school after thanking me for my help in a tone that conveyed enough filial solicitude to inspire the security that comes to a parent when he knows his child is wise.

Among other things, the day's schedule called for me to descend to the bottom of a swimming pool in a sponge-diver's suit to do a bit on an NBC network show. The suit had been borrowed from an old Greek diver from Tarpon Springs, who told me that they nearly all leaked, and not to worry until it got pretty full of water.

When I did a test in it the day before without broadcasting equipment, I noted that it took three full minutes to have the helmet set properly on the neck ring, and to have each bolt tightened with a wrench.

I went down and got the hang of discharging air from

a valve which was activated by knocking my head against a button inside the helmet. Everything went fine. Even if the compressor failed I was only a few steps from a ladder and safety. The only thing that bothered me was that if the helmet filled with water I could not hold my breath for as long as it took them to bolt the helmet on, and I might gain the distinction of being the first man to drown on dry land.

On the day of the show I got back into the suit. The only difference this time was that the wires for my microphone and the headset I wore were arranged along my arm and came out at the wrist. This created a leak. If I held my right hand down, water came in as air went out the helmet valve. To hold my right arm higher than the helmet meant that air went out, but that was all right since air was being pumped into the suit constantly. But water that had been accumulating in the sleeve was then dumped into the legs of the suit. In this manner I pumped water into the suit, which filled it faster than it would have filled from its several leaks.

My headset was wired so that I got something different in each ear. In my left I heard the program as it was being aired, and in my right I got instructions from the program director.

When the switch was made to me from a location forty miles away—a department store, from which Arlene Francis was to carry on a conversation with me—I was just descending into the pool. Attached to the headset was my microphone—a telephone transmitter such as operators use.

The air being pumped to me smelled of gasoline and rubber. And it kept coming whether I wanted it or not. As the suit began to balloon, I tried to knock my head against the escape valve in the helmet, but found I couldn't because of the headset, which I hadn't worn when I'd made my test run. As more and more air came in, my arms began to rise. The final stage of this unhappy fix is that the diver is spread-eagled, and the helmet eventually slips off over his head, letting him down inside the suit where he can't possibly get at the valve. In time the buoyancy overcomes the weight of the lead belt and shoes and everything comes to the surface like a cork.

I turned my head several different ways trying for the right position. Finally I found one that allowed me to push on the valve. As the air rushed out of the suit, my arms came back down. Through the suit I could feel the water tighten around me.

During this maneuver I was silent until I heard Arlene's voice.

"Are you all right?" she said.

"Yes," I said, "I'm fine."

"Move to your right," I heard the director saying in the other ear. I started to walk. It was very lumbering, and had to be done with bent knees.

"Do you see any sponges?" Arlene asked.

"Uh—no. No sponges," I replied, "but there are pennies in the water. They're floating down."

"He's flipped," came the director's voice. "He thinks he sees pennies floating down."

"I do!" I said. "I think kids at the edge of the pool are throwing them." I moved further to the right. When I tried to look down I discovered the suit was too full of air again. I moved my head to the valve and shoved. Air rushed out.

"—like to stay down there for a few hours?" Arlene's voice was saying.

"No," I said, "not till they start throwing quarters."

Now my right sleeve was heavy with water. I lifted it, and as the air rushed out, the accumulated water ran into the suit and part way down the legs. Part way, because there was already water nearly to the crotch.

"I think the suit's filling with water," I said.

"You'd better stop it, you silly bastard," came Schneider's voice again, "you've got awhile to go down there."

"I'm not doing it," I said, and instantly realized I'd been talking to him as well as Arlene.

"Not doing what?" Arlene asked. "Are you sure you're all right?"

After some unsuccessful attempts to stoop over and pick up some of the pennies (let's face it—they were the only things of interest on the bottom of that pool), what with the suit ballooning and shipping water constantly, and the danger of my saying at any moment what I was hearing from Schneider, I announced that I was ready to come out.

"I haven't got the limbo shot yet!" Schneider shrieked. He was referring to a trick he'd rigged for getting a shot presumably from under the surface. This was done by parking an empty helmet behind a small fish tank through which the shot was to be made. Bubbles were rising in the tank as a stage manager blew through a drinking straw. The effect, with my voice clanking from inside my own helmet, was of his having submerged a camera to get a close-up view of me.

While I stood still and talked about sponges, and of other things the suit owner had told me about his profession, I couldn't help wondering why *he* wasn't down here doing this. It was hard to keep from saying what I could hear Schneider saying. I was now waist-high in water inside the suit and it was rising, minute by minute.

When they finally pulled me up and unbolted me, the old Greek told me divers usually stay down until the water is close to the helmet. Then they signal to be brought up.

18
A Deal With Reality

THERE IS SOMETHING about television that bends conversations toward statements of philosophy. The statements may be disguised, or they may be hidden in humor and lighthearted banter, but that is the direction the talk takes on conversation shows, if it is not consciously guided away. The burlesque queen will have something to say about juvenile delinquency, the guest political analyst will itch to air his theory of esthetics, the comic will thread his way through one-liners to zero in on something profound about friendship or justice.

There are many reasons for this. The occasion of appearing on television is flavored with gravity unless a different mood is very carefully established. A sense of the commercial value of the time, the idea that just being there, on the air, is of importance—this sobers all but the most seasoned guests, who alone are able to be as relaxed as if they were, literally, in their own or your living room.

The question remains, why, when tempered and impressed, does the guest chafe to gush his nicest insights and his entire body of doctrine? One theory is that we must all make some sort of deal with reality, and a statement of personal philosophy can be a marshalling and reviewing of our defenses. Some people trot out their little armies with pride, and thump each soldier on the chest in passing—others offer theirs in shame and terror, as though their inner peace is threatened simply by being reminded of what a shaky and pathetic force stands between them and a hostile cosmos. Many, apologetic about their garrisons, find themselves in the gallant but ludicrous position of defending their defenses. But in any case, public appearance seems to many to be a time for having defenses ready to account—hence the tendency to state personal philosophy.

For a reason I have no desire to trace, I seem to have this same effect on people in conversation, when they are prone to air their deepest principles and opinions to me. It may be because I appear to listen wisely. It is a habit of mine to listen as though I were bringing wisdom as well as interest to what is being said. I wish I were. The real trick is to talk wisely, but that's a horse of a different shade. Silence never has the effect of proving you're a fool—it tends to do the opposite. At least it has the effect of encouraging people to let their hair down. This is one facet of psychiatric technique. I don't know that anyone feels better after talking to me, but I often feel I've learned something more than facts about the person.

I have listened to people who thought everything was wrong in the world and to a few who thought everything was right. For example, a young chap with a public relations firm, had (still has) a euphoric, almost pathological optimism. It serves him well in his work. The experience he related to me at some length in a bar on Forty-ninth Street showed the extent to which he was preoccupied with the "rightness of each moment," as he called it.

"This girl wasn't more than fifty feet away when I first saw her," Red was explaining. "She was sitting on the bench by the wall. All this went through my mind in the time it took to reach her." He was turning his glass between his thumb and second finger, and the way he paused and looked at the ice cubes showed he was aware of the rightness of the moment.

"It was early fall," he went on. "Still summer, as far as temperature went, but the air seemed thinner and the sun brighter and the leaves had begun to fade like they do before they turn. Everything seemed right, if you know what I mean. And then I see her, sitting there reading a book. So immediately I think, 'Suddenly it's even more right.' She looks pretty good, you see. Now, step by step I try to imagine what will improve this day. First, I say to myself, it would certainly be improved if I sit beside this chick and strike it off in friendly fashion. You follow?"

"Gladly," I said. "But it looks like trouble."

"Wait till you hear. I figure this can only be an improvement if she isn't waiting to meet some bruiser she's engaged to or married to—that'd pretty much mash the whole thing. So I supposed, since I was making this up as I went along that such was not the case—that she was unattached. Suddenly the day seemed brighter. Something had been added. Obviously.

"I then thought—and by now I wasn't more than ten feet closer—I mean I'd only walked about ten more feet—the mind works like lightning, you know."

"Especially when it's doping out a way to make it with—"

"No, any thoughts go charging around inside the skull without wasting much time. So—now I figure what could make this day even more complete. Naturally you know the answer. I figured that if in striking up an acquaintance she felt about me like I was already sure I was going to feel about her—why, you know, we'd be in the sack before sundown."

I could see how the moment was getting righter.

"There is, however, more to life when it comes to plumbing depths than frothy encounters such as I was imagining." He drained some water from the bottom of his glass and looked for the bartender. "So in seeking to perfect the day I had to look beyond the immediate need gratification and face the fact that deep down what we all want is love—to express it and receive it—and that if an affair is free of entanglements, like we prefer, it's also free of love, and then it's nowhere and we wind up judging such a girl as less than feminine. By now I'm about thirty feet from her and asking myself again, what would make things more perfect. Well, I figured that if my conversation with her indicated right off that I was heading toward being really in love with her—I don't mean lying about it, but really feeling that way—I would then be entitled to a reciprocal feeling from her. But I needed something more."

"Yes," I said as the bartender came toward us. "Someone to pull you off the street with a net."

"We'll have the same," Red told the bartender, who nodded and turned away. "There!" said Red, "did you see how right that was? The way he nodded then—couldn't have been more perfect for the moment! Where was I? Oh—yes. By now, in my imagination, I'm deeply in love with this girl, and she's on the way to being deeply in love with me. Now what is love? True love?"

This was about the heaviest question ever leveled at me in broad daylight, so I just blinked.

"True love," Red said slowly, as though I'd said it first and he was repeating it to show he was proud of me, "is a sharing of your complete self with the object of your love. And what is your complete self but the sum total of all your experiences? Something more was needed now and quick. I'm only twenty feet from this girl, and in love with her, and as such duty-bound to share my entire self, which as you know includes a wife and three children."

Our drinks were brought, and I thanked the bartender.

"That was very Zen," Red said, "the way you thanked him."

"Zen Buddhist?"

"Yes. It was right for the moment."

"But I mumbled."

"Doesn't matter. It was perfect."

Red Merriam had a way of making you feel as though you'd accomplished something for no good reason at all. I had apparently done something quite difficult. Zen Buddhism was (in my mind and at that time) in the custody of beatniks except for Red, and the few beatniks I knew indicated that it was pretty hard to understand.

"So now," Red went on, "if I plan to tell her about the wife and children it's got to have some effect. She will either reject me or she'll say it doesn't make any difference, she'll take whatever of my love she can get and won't complain. If she says the latter then it's my duty to end it. By renouncing her."

"Renouncing?"

"That's the proper term. And if she rejects me, then I've left the burden of ending it with her. That would mar the rightness. So you see in either case I've got to renounce her. For her sake and mine and the family and, for that matter, for the universe. The rightness, you know." He took a long pull at his drink. He deserved it.

"Now," he continued, "to end a day like that one with a jarring thing like a renunciation, after what we'd meant to each other—that would hardly be right—at least it would lack perfection. It would lack perfection for another and more important reason: if I did it well, it would make her love me more, in view of the nobility of the action. You see? It would sort of fan the flames. So something was needed to make the situation better. You've probably guessed what it was."

"No, I haven't." I looked at him and then took a drink myself. I felt I might need it for the rightness of the next few moments. "What?"

"I needed what seemed for a moment like the impossible: A renunciation that wasn't a renunciation. Now there is such a thing. It has a real Zen flavor and I found it, and the day was perfect!" He stood there grinning.

I stared at him, determined not to ask him directly what this renunciation that was not a renunciation looked like, or sounded like, and at the same time wondering if he would think that someone kicking him in the fanny would be right for the moment.

"It came to me when I was ten feet from her. On the top of all the words and actions—the very pinnacle of the passion and the long plot of meeting, falling in love, the exaltedness of loving deeply enough to make a lie intolerable and finding it necessary to give each other up and return to duty—and somehow to accomplish this without the hurt that would have to follow any consciousness of having done it—the very crowning act that would accomplish this very thing came to me in a flash!"

"And it was the right thing for the moment?"

"It was perfect!" He leaned closer. "I decided to walk past her without looking at her at all! And I *did* it!"

I had to admit it was about the Zennest thing I'd ever heard of, and I imagined everybody including Red's wife would admit it made the day perfect.

To keep this one perfect I settled up and went home. It seemed just right for the moment.

The other extreme is just as interesting and probably shows a greater tendency to cling to illusions.

But it can be brought out by a broadcast just as surely as optimism. This is one reason the Jack Paar show actually reveals more of the real self in a guest than you would find if you spent an hour and three-quarters alone with him.

I used to think people who saw the worst in any situation were disillusioned. I realize now that it would kill them to be parted from their illusions. They, more than the others, need to cling to their own attitude.

Rumwell Dantas clings to an attitude that may serve him satisfactorily, but it is nothing to bolster the general morale of anyone else I know. Rumwell seems to have been robbed at birth of his natural share of hope. He has been a doorman in a building on Park Avenue for twenty-five years. Everything about the world is hopeless to him. It's a view you can't combat logically beyond a certain point, because healthy outlooks and wills-to-live are not rationally-arrived-at things; so every bit of news, every single situation of daily living vindicates his stand.

If there has been a bad local traffic mishap or a head-lined plane crash it is never a surprise to him. It's as though he has been solemnly waiting for the word to be brought.

If it is raining you sense Rumwell's appreciation of the

propriety of the situation. If the sun shines, he will offer the weather bureau's prediction of the next bad weather as triumphant proof that all good things are short-lived and as a result, treacherous, since they bring about a false hope and a heady frivolity in humankind.

If a tenant leaves the building with luggage Rumwell never misses the chance to express the hope they aren't flying "in this weather." Once he said this to a young executive on the prettiest June day New York had seen in years.

"Rummy, this is a perfect day for flying!" the man said.

"Yes," Rummy flung back, "and it can change like *that!*" and he snapped his fingers to show how fate can close in on those who seek escape by picking favorable times to trick the gods.

We got to know Rumwell Dantas through friends who lived in his building. Once when we had the children with us he said to Ruth and me after they'd gone ahead into the lobby, "They're happy children, aren't they?" We said yes they were.

"Poor things," he said. "They don't know."

"Good Lord, Rumwell," I said, "don't know what?"

He never explained, as though it would be embarrassing to explain the obvious, or as though if *we* didn't understand, we too were so deluded he could never reach us.

To Rumwell Life is a gloomy corridor along which we are all pushed by the big hand of Time and at the end of which is the embalmer. This is his illusion, his something solid. Plainly he has chosen a position from which he can't fall. From his rock-bottom outlook, any degree of being wrong can only be gravy. His motto for action and personal spiritual commitment is "Nothing ventured nothing lost." And though his aspect may be considered blighted and hideous, he is remarkably well adjusted. Since things are constantly as bad as he can make them, nothing can change for the worse. What optimist can say this about his own world?

If the range of human methods of dealing with reality were scalar, we'd all fit somewhere between Red Merriman and Rumwell Dantas—between the rightness of every moment and the wrongness. But human methods, particularly those not dominated by intellectual motivation, do not locate themselves in a one-dimensional continuum. The emotions are infinite. Logic itself may derive its structure and substance from emotional needs. A rationalization, after all, is not rational.

As a result, few of life's raw and dangerous forces are tempered purely by the intellect. Ambition itself may be controlled by a stoic quality that is not the fruit of any study of stoicism, however ardent. And such ambition can wind up at very different goals.

I knew a man whose philosophy and life demonstrated this. He used to visit the studios occasionally when I was working the sign-off shift at WLOK in Lima. And because I listened to him, he reacted as he might have in a broadcast studio. He laid out his philosophy.

Alston Blackwell had turned his education, which was probably not as complete as he made it sound, but nevertheless impressive, toward polishing a line of thought that formed a clear arrow pointed in a clear direction if you listened to him long enough. I would be typewriting logs and making schedules and pulling records during incoming net feeds at the station, and so had ample exposure to the Blackwell lectures. I sometimes wondered what he was doing in Lima, Ohio.

He was about fifty, nearly bald and quite stooped. His mother, who was still living, was wealthy enough to have set him up with a sporting goods store six or eight years before. This enterprise he had run straight into the ground. One night he more or less told me his life's story.

"When I was five years old I wanted more than anything to be an elevator operator," he said dreamily. "The idea of motion in a vertical shaft at the thrust of a lever was the most thrilling thing I could think of." It seemed a complicated thrill for a five-year-old, but I didn't say anything.

"There was an Otis in the Demarest Building in New York then," he said, taking a cigarette from a gold case he carried, and then offering one to me. "My Uncle Horace let me ride up and down with the operator—I suppose to keep me out from under foot." He smiled and lit his cigarette.

"Then I must have been nine or so when I watched the foreman of a construction gang shouting orders at a group of men. And I suddenly realized that we are not islands in this world. There are others to deal with and to work with, and the zest of life must surely spring from assuming authority and reaping the consequences of your own action, so to speak. Casting yourself on the block and accepting the blame or praise, but all the while seeing something take shape before your eyes. Something you've directed. This was the thing to be—a foreman with a building outfit." He put his feet up on the open drawer of a transcription file cabinet and looked at the ceiling. I went on typing.

"But you outgrow dreams of action. There are two reasons for the very young thinking in terms of physical action. One is the abundance of energy in growing bodies —almost a need to waste it. The other is a lack of awareness of the mental activity going on behind the scenes on higher levels that determine what physical action will take place. Construction gangs never sink a spade until someone has decided to spend the money."

He was warming up. The long pause that followed was not an invitation for me to urge him on, but rather a trunnion on which he might pivot his next observation.

"I must have been sixteen or seventeen when I made up my mind to head a large corporation. Here would be the ultimate satisfaction, I said to myself. A manufacturing concern providing products to a free people, and employment to a sizable community. I finished high school early, and had a flare for business. My father wanted to put me in Harvard, but I felt I could achieve a goal faster by cutting through the liberal arts aspects of standard curricula. I begged him to let me attend a business school." Alston flicked an ash on the carpeting. "And then —" he paused again and at length shook his head. "I saw a still higher goal."

He took his feet off the file drawer and stood up. "I decided even to skip business school for this one." He paced to the water cooler and back to the file drawer, smiling as one does when recollections send up fumes of past folly and tenderness. "To be, I reasoned, a manipulator of money—big money—other people's money—this must be the summit—the very pinnacle of life."

"Why would you skip business school?" I asked, feeling it might be rude not to say anything at all.

"Because, my boy, the school of hard knocks is the one for that kind of life. You don't need Harvard for social connections, because when you start dealing in money in six figures and up, you find you make connections very fast. The social register suddenly falls open for you. And you don't need formal business training above what you pick up by working for an investment banking firm. I had a chance to get into Francis I. DuPont on Wall Street through Uncle Horace. The job, frankly, was office boy. But many a tycoon has risen from just that position to dominate vast holdings."

He took a long drag on his cigarette, looking hard at me. "If you go out on a limb, go *way* out. If you get yourself in personal debt for a few thousand dollars, you'll get an ulcer worrying about it. So avoid that. Get yourself in debt for many thousands, or if possible, millions, and you don't have worries. You may never be able to pay it back, but you will have established a living standard—a luxurious one, and you'll find you have a fantastic kind of credit."

I watched him grind out his cigarette on the rug and sink again into his chair.

"I found," he said, putting his hands behind his head and looking again at the ceiling, "a more exalted goal."

I gave up on the log, took the sheet out of the typewriter and leaned forward onto it with my chin on my fist. He resumed.

"Financial manipulation is fine if you like it. It has a certain effect on the lives of many people, but it has its limitations. There are things in life that can't be bought."

I thought perhaps he had at this point determined to go into the ministry. I said, "Yes. I believe that."

"If you are really going to be a force for good in this world, you can't quite make it by controlling money, in whatever quantities. Government and law are the fields for being a real force and politics is the tool. A legal background is essential here. If a man did no more with his life than serve in office in some way that furthered the American Ideal however slightly, and buttressed the country against inroads of subversive ideologies, he'd have reward enough."

"I suppose," I said, "but the living standard doesn't go with it, if you play fair. Honest statesmanship isn't a wealthy—"

"Of course not," Blackwell said. "What is wealth? If you have millions, what do you really own? Society is a system of laws that must protect the common good, and that automatically entails regulations that make ownership meaningless. Why not live modestly with the knowledge that the force you exert is significant and right?" He took his feet off the drawer and leaned forward, elbows on knees. "I decided to seek public office."

"Great," I said. It was all I could think of at the moment. "Did you study law for that?"

"I was going to. And I would have except for one thing."

I stared at him. "You found a goal higher than this?"

"I did." He rose, but instead of pacing, held out his arms sideways, smiling. He dropped them with a slap against his legs as though he had explained everything.

"I made a study on my own," he said at last, "of the lives of great men—really great men. And I noticed a singular feature they all shared. They never attempted to influence vast numbers of people directly. Socrates, Gautama Buddha, Jesus of Nazareth. All of them influenced only those around them. They were content with their immediate environment and their span of life. They sought no memorials, because they were in touch with the infinite and eternal."

"So?"

"So that became my goal. To give up wealth and power in favor of influencing, I hope for good, those around me. I don't think of myself as really great, don't get me wrong, but I'd rather be a small great man than a great small man, if you follow me. The man pushing big sums of money around for narrow or selfish reasons is a small man, really, who is pretending to be great. I'd rather be a small man really acting—sincerely I mean—as I think a great man would act—do you follow this?"

"I think so."

"Many of those great ones in history sponged unabashedly from disciples. I don't say there's anything wrong with that, but it's awkward in this day and age, and unless you avoid it you may not be listened to at all. So I decided that some kind of work was necessary, just to pay my own way so to speak. And that work should be menial in character, because it doesn't absorb your attention and divert you from higher thoughts, and because a humble job is the best way of serving others. Again, in small numbers."

I suddenly realized Blackwell had achieved his ambition —his final goal. Either that, or here was the most towering rationalization I was apt to run across in all my days.

"Was that the bell?" he asked, cocking his head.

"It sounded like it."

He started out. "Probably the cleaning woman on nine. She leaves earlier than the others." He readjusted his cap on his head. "Thanks for the chat," he said.

"Not at all. Gets kind of lonesome here anyway."

"You think about what I said." He turned as the bell sounded again. "Keep your shirt on!" he yelled to his elevator, the door of which he had propped open, "I'll be there!"

19
What Is Anyone Really Like?

IN JULY OF 1957 I called Jack Paar at his home to ask him if he would be a guest interview on a show I was doing for vacationing Tex and Jinx. Jack and I had never met, but he had at that time agreed to fill the breach for NBC's last-gasp attempt at late-night live TV; and he had asked for me to announce the show. I thought I could get a newsworthy guest and at the same time become acquainted with the star of the new Tonight show (later to be called the Jack Paar show, although he still calls it "Tonight.")

During our phone conversation he said, "The kids in my neighborhood kick sand in my pool. I have to clean it out." The reason for his saying this was probably simply that he thought of it. It had no clear connection with what we were talking about, but something reminded him of it, so he blurted it out. This transparency and candor has brought on several lawsuits and a trip to Hong Kong as well as the vital force of the most fascinating program on television.

He accepted the invitation, incidentally, and was an

excellent and witty guest. I was impressed with his courage when he outlined some of his ideas for this new late-night venture. They seemed bold and somewhat unorthodox. I wish I could report that I foresaw in them the success of the show. The truth is, I suspected deep down that within a few weeks NBC would be running old movies late at night.

Jack weeded out ideas that weren't sound, including some of his own, and stuck to his guns; and within a month the Tonight show lumbered shuddering into the air, gaining enough altitude in two years that the nose dive of his walkout wrought no lasting harm.

So much comment has been made on Paar—ranging from the sloppy whitewash of the vapid and obsequious to boiling-acid streams from the ulcerous and variously wounded—that the addition of my comments would be wearily redundant except that there are things about Jack Paar and his program which need clarifying as long as the question keeps popping up: What is he really like?

The press has in general been sketchy about these things and in some cases has slanted its reports unfairly in avenging its own injuries.

No broadcast on the air to my knowledge makes such a careful separation of real from theatrical as does the Paar show. The principal technique of his effecting this has cost him his acceptance by the cognoscenti. The insiders of the communications business have put him outside. He violated two rules of a sort of gentlemen's code: (1) He attacked the press through an upstart medium; (2) He presented himself to the public with fantastic honesty—faults and all. "Showbiz" just doesn't do this and television was thought to be showbiz. The clown must laugh, they say, even if he feels like crying, and the show must go on. But here is a clown who cries when he feels like crying, whose laughter as a result is genuine, and who feels there are worse things in the world than the show's not going on. One of them is not to show one's true self. The broadcast personality who distinguishes nicely between a fault and a virtue will be careful to hide the one and display the other. In doing this he is less honest than Jack Paar. The anguish of those who profess dislike for Paar yet watch him faithfully is rooted in the discomfort of seeing their own human traits amplified by a mass medium and audaciously mirrored at them. I submit that those most distressed are those with the most to hide from themselves.

It has often been said in print, and Jack himself sometime gives the appearance on the air, that he is overalert and edgily self-protective, sensitive about his own feelings and careless about the feelings of others, uncertain of his own taste and judgment, lacking in tolerance of the shortcomings of others, prone to rob guests of their dignity, retaliative, petulant and unpredictable.

His reaction to audiences and street crowds seems to indicate a certain dread of his fellow humans in large numbers. He suspects and sometimes misinterprets friendly advances. People who get along best with him are those who remain somewhat aloof. This limits and defines friends, and probably causes some loneliness.

But for every criticism of an action or attitude of Jack's one could cite an action or attitude opposite in character. The frankness with which he presents all sides of himself results in spotlighting faults and eclipsing virtues. Let's look at some of the latter:

Every just critical remark offered without bitterness gets through to him for a thoughtful reception. He has either already acknowledged it or will take it to heart and try to learn from it. Vengeance comes into play only when the criticism is barbed or flavored with rancor, or factually untrue. His retaliation at least follows the talion law. He lashes out irresponsibly only at irresponsible lashings-out.

He is genuinely happy at the success of others. I have watched this at close range. For some reason, this is seldom remarked of him, although I believe this comes through on the air to a certain extent. He tempers his beliefs often in favor of a friend. The closest he comes to dishonesty is in giving a better review to someone's play or work of art than he feels it really deserves, in order to help it. This is compassion. He is genuinely distressed at the genuine distress of others—sometimes inordinately. He took to calling me Malcolm a couple of years ago, as a result of exploring the middle names of all the guests on one night's show. (His middle name is Harold.) The "Malcolm" sort of stuck. It was a friendly gesture on his part, like a nickname, and would probably have lasted indefinitely except for my mentioning one night that it bothered a relative of mine whose father's first name had provided my middle name. It couldn't have mattered less, really, but Jack was disturbed that it had upset my cousin and I believe he thought it bothered me. (It's possible it did or I might not have mentioned it at all.) Anyway he said he would never call me Malcolm again and somehow he has managed it to this day without a lapse. Guests have walked away from the show in tears at some real or imagined cruelty, but I have seen a whole show ruined for Jack because he had unintentionally done some hurt to a visitor—or thought he had.

With the possible exception of Irv Kupcinet in Chicago, Jack Paar has a greater talent for bringing out the real personality of people than any other interviewer I have seen. The difference between the two is that in Irv's interviews he allows the real personality of his guests to emerge at their leisure. Jack drags the real (and sometimes reluctant) personality from a guest in relatively short order (he never has more than six minutes before it's time for another commercial). This can be frightening, and I sympathize with any star who doesn't want to face it. The Paar show is no place for the timid, nor for those who preen a fragile dignity and carry it to the theater in the belief it will be put on a pedestal and viewed from its best angle. It is more likely to be sat on or used as a football.

But I can truthfully say that I believe, after seven hundred hours on this nightly nut-meet, that anyone who comes off looking bad is himself solely responsible for it. Jack Paar has never made anyone look bad. Nobody can make anyone else look bad. A guest on a show can be neglected, misused, even abused, but if he looks bad, he has done it to himself. I have never known Jack to gloss over the situation if a guest has come on loaded. He won't bail him out by hoodwinking the viewers. In a celebrated case a mildly loaded guest dug himself thirty feet into the ground in as many minutes and later wanted to sue. A staff member remarked, "How can you sue someone for watching you make a fool of yourself?"

Once years ago I saw a TV cooking show on which the chef accidentally ripped a piece of aluminum foil while trying to wrap a fish, and made a valiant effort to hide the fact. This kind of dishonesty is pathetic and embarrassing, even to the viewer, and it is death to a show. When that Eye has seen something, no amount of piety or wit can call back a single subliminal flash. A lie about it is not a white lie—it is a muddy, smelly little lie. There is no furtive hiding of such a thing by Jack Paar. If you guest on his show and rip your foil, he is most apt to say, breezily, "You ripped your foil!"

This has led to a role on my part of sometime devil's advocate. I defend things and people from time to time simply to make certain more than one side of an issue is aired. But the role is tricky and a little presumptious. Often my reason for urging Jack not to lash out is that he can boost his intended victim by giving him valuable publicity and at the same time doing himself harm. He acknowledges this argument but continues periodically to aim his blowgun and then suck poison darts from it into his own throat.

I think all of us, like Jack, have this impulse to repay a wrong, but unlike Jack, we haven't the instant openness that results in televising every impulse. He who delays action until he has cooled down can give the impression he was never steamed up in the first place.

The extent to which the Paar show has been an instrument of free speech and to which Jack has been a champion of free speech has never been given adequate emphasis. It is not simply that he speaks freely and has invaded areas of custom, politics, morals and religion hitherto tacitly taboo except in certain circumscribed and somber settings by certain qualified and somber people. He has passed the test of taking pains to see that someone gets a chance to be heard, even knowing what is to be said will cut across a tenet of his own or will cause him some embarrassment. This kind of embarrassment is *not* a lie and gives life to a show.

A famous star came on one night and asked to flatten a national magazine which had printed something unpleasant about her. The magazine had just been extremely kind to Jack in a cover story and he would certainly have been more comfortable to have a guest praise it than blast it, but he invited the star to say what she pleased.

He has created a national spotlight that is brighter—from the standpoint of press space, public conversation and the developing of new talent—than anything else in television. He has pushed many people into that light—people who have furthered their careers and personal fortunes and enterprises and tax shelters far more than he has. To my knowledge he's never taken a dime of loot, nor sold the power of his office, nor promoted outside personal interests beyond his book (which he's mentioned less than the books of any regular guest) nor countenanced any shabby ethics in the way of plugs. He takes no orders and scarcely any direction. He loves people but hates crowds. (The reverse is more in the tradition of this business.) He admits to meager talent as a comedian but he is undeniably a wit. He is a Republican who gets enthusiastic about Jack Kennedy. He is the idol of millions and a source of unfathomed irritation to hundreds of thousands. He is really like that. And that's the answer to the question what is he really like.

We have recently felt the need of and created a new type of celebrity—a human. We have demanded on the one hand that we no longer be fooled—that our TV fare make a rigorous separation of theatrical entertainment from genuine human situations.

But on the other hand, when we get exactly what we asked for, we wince. Some of us recoil. We wonder, momentarily, whether the skeleton should have been brought out of the closet. So we turn from the childlike frankness of an untheatrical star who doesn't bother with cautious protocol and cliché custom—but only for a moment. We turn back to look at him, because we want to look at ourselves and we know about John Donne's bell.

Watching that nightly parade of personalities undergoing vivisection on TV's rifest broadcast, we are slowly going toward an answer to the question: "What is humanity really like?"

20

Cogitations of a Broadcaster

TEN YEARS AGO a definition of television was "an electronic miracle that hurls images through the air so that you may sit in your home and watch a movie you didn't go to see fifteen years ago because it wasn't any good."

The gestation period of this incredible infant was a long one. For television was conceived at approximately the same time as radio. The first effective transmission of a picture was in 1921. It was born, as a commercial possibility, after World War II. The stepchild of radio, it seemed to fight for itself in those early days, developing a zest and vigor that sometimes grows in a child which senses that it isn't wanted. In many quarters television wasn't wanted. Big-time broadcasting people were radio people, and when their budgets were cut into by clients withdrawing advertising money to try the new medium, there were hard feelings.

More and more sets were sold, until soon there were more TV sets than bathtubs in America, and the infant had more strength than it knew what to do with. In short succession it went through its stages of circuses, wrestling and used-car dealers, and quickly entered a lavish phase of reckless production. It began to visit out of the way spots across America, moving whole towns for reasons of its own (once a director in Washington ordered a grave marker in Arlington Cemetery to be moved because it was in the way of a shot he wanted for a national TV show). It toppled the movie industry and then spared that giant's life by having it make movies for television. After discovering Americans' thirst for Americana, it spawned a rash of Westerns that Bret Harte could never have dreamed of in the lushest days of the dime novel. It revived the money games of radio days, dressed them in gaudy trappings and played fast and loose with the public faith. In effect, it filled its medicine bottles at the river, got caught, and was tarred and feathered. Whether or not it is chastened at present, it is certainly cautious, probably thoughtful. I believe it to be settling on a run of improved entertainment, genuine public service, and a willingness to be steered by respectability.

That these are the motives of the people in control of TV is not so important as the fact that the industry must shape up in a way acceptable to the public which supports it. And no matter how cloudy and inarticulate the public's morality, that morality is there. There may be setbacks, but in time they melt away. The direction is forward.

Some of the setbacks appear to be discouragingly hardy. The difficulty young television got itself into was only a part of a broader difficulty that eats at us as a nation. This disease has resulted in frauds and investigations ranging from labor racketeering through cranberry packing, meat weighing and disc jockeys, to corruption in high public office. In a causal chain, the sudden public awareness and righteous indignation derive from the findings of investigating committees and the confessions of those implicated. These in turn stem from the natural, inevitable exploiting of situations rooted in materialism—from the callousness of our Horatio Alger glorification of grasping thrift and ruthless ambition. The beaver skins that could not be exhausted but somehow ran out; the technical supremacy in which we took such pride and then took for granted until the other side of the moon was photographed by somebody else; the subtle shift of our national faith from God to Mammon; and the resultant reward of a record incidence of alcoholism, divorce, suicide, delinquency and mental breakdown—these are unconscious forms of disillusion that are forcing us to investigate, to take stock, to probe, to wake up.

It is not too late to tap those values we thought we'd outgrown. I don't mean to say that a maudlin return to these old values, useful during the reign of Queen Victoria, would benefit the Space Age. Rather, what I would suggest is a careful reappraisal of old values and basic concepts. This could be done by a group of scientifically grounded philosophers, known to be objective and dispassionate, and chosen by a populace whose level of education has been elevated. Elevated sufficiently to dispense with the suspicion so characteristic of democracy when it attempts to function at low educational levels.

To set up such a body of philosopher-rulers (or even philosopher-advisers) and expect a society such as ours to trust it and tolerate it is Utopian. It is still too popular to hate the "egghead."

Education alone can lead us out of this morass. And education cannot do it in a single generation. There is no medium better suited to this task than television. It must convey faithfully the truths of our own time and the salvageable, applicable values of older moral standards. At the same time it should popularize newer concepts by the exposure of certain ideas that must no longer be ignored: (1) Wasting energy in race hatred is fatal. (2) Intelligence is not dangerous. (Even off the leash of a university faculty.) (3) Communist Russia and the situation its plans embody merit our respect and constant alertness and the avoidance of shortsighted reaction. "In our association with Russia," writes F. S. C. Northrop in his book *The Meeting of East and West*, we must be realistic, becoming perfectly clear in our minds concerning precisely what their theory is, avoiding at all costs opportunistic reactions based on a sentimental mood of repulsion at one moment or of brotherly love and attraction at another moment." (4) We will not be saved from present or future dangers by narrow nationalism but only by a sense of freedom vital enough to help us adapt to new and changing conditions.

The sorriest aspect of the TV quiz scandals was that television appeared to its public to have been in the hands of unprincipled opportunists. To the extent that this may have heightened distrust of the medium and of things intellectual, it was even more damaging than it immediately appeared to be. One cannot blame people for regarding it warily for some time to come. I'm all for this wariness on an indefinite basis. The real crime of the quiz frauds is that it damaged one of the best channels for straightening out cultural warps through education—television.

Continuing damage of a different kind is still being done by overcontrol of program content by advertisers footing the bill. TV writer Rod Serling has said, "The sponsors are afraid to show a minority group, afraid to take a single stand even if that stand shows that prejudice is bad. . . . It gets down to this: Be careful of any group with a slate of officers and a letterhead—The American Legion, The American Medical Society, The American Dental Society, The Spam Marching and Chowder Society of Retired Officers. A sponsor is very aware of all these groups that write letters, and is very intimidated by them."

So far this control appears to be of a negative type. It seems to be a system of avoidance, wherein the sponsor will not run a risk of being linked to anything that might be controversial, even to what might *become* controversial. I have to say, in defense of the participating-sponsor format of shows I've worked in recent years—Home, Concentration, the Jack Paar show—that there has been no hint of interference from sponsors regarding what I should or should not say on the air. But it is true that even the positive statement of an enlightened viewpoint frightens sponsors who are the sole commercial entity on a show.

Sponsors are not alone in this. Studios, networks, production agencies, all tend to shy away from any firm stand on any issue. And strangely enough, sometimes organizations whose sole and stated aim is to spread an enlightened view can stand in the way of that view. It does not, to my thinking, help to reduce racial bigotry to deny that this country was a slave country at one time. And yet the NBC historic-adventure series "Riverboat," in one episode of which I played a role, did not once cast a Negro in any part whatever. The production unit was not discriminating against, it was discriminating for. Wouldn't it be wonderful if we could erase that blot on our shield of liberty—if we could change the fact of the horror of slavery by simply denying it now? Of course we can't do it, and in trying we are doing the very thing for which we condemn the Communists. We are rewriting history.

The future must bring to TV not only the character of mercy and fair play, but of strength.

This strength, I believe, will come from television's own potential. It can and will link cities together in massive closed-circuit telecasts, allowing legislators in local communities to participate in national legislative sessions.

Television promises to strengthen the democratic ideal in more ways than one. First, by the linking together of local units of larger organizations—business and legislative. Second, by informing factually. And third, by enjoining the people to know themselves. It is causing the nation to look on its own face by introducing a new kind of celebrity—the Ordinary Person whose special talent is being himself in front of millions.

These strange celebrities are celebrated because they are widely known—there is no other real reason. They may incidentally amuse, or instruct, or appeal to instincts base or exalted. They may be relaxed or crew cut or pleasant, or appear dependable and steadfast. They may display fretfulness, bad temper, rebellion, weakness and illness— we are all heir to these shortcomings. They may be caricatures, but as such they are pungent artistic distortions of something true; they slam home a truth. While we may find their public indulgence of emotions a sharp and shocking breach of tradition, we must remember that we watch them through a medium which has no tradition as yet.

The advent of television—the full flowering of radio broadcasting—is ultimately of more importance to the human race than the Industrial Revolution, the splitting or fusing of the atom, or the development of cybernetics and automation; it has more immediate impact on society than psychiatry. TV is here, now, in millions of homes, having become a daily habit with vast and far-reaching consequences not yet correctly assayed by the networks, the broadcasters, the Federal Communications Commission, or the public.

Television can do much for this nation. And once established as a world-wide communications network, it will realize its potential for peace among all nations.